TO ASPEN AND BACK

TO ASPEN AND BACK
An American Journey

PEGGY CLIFFORD

ST. MARTIN'S PRESS
175 FIFTH AVENUE · NEW YORK

Grateful acknowledgement is made for permission to reprint:
Quotation from *A Lost Lady*, by Willa Cather. Copyright 1923 by
Willa S. Cather and renewed 1951 by Edith Lewis, Executrix and
City Bank Farmers Trust Co., Reprinted by permission of Alfred
A. Knopf, Inc.

Excerpt from article by Alexander Cockburn. Reprinted by
permission of Alexander Cockburn and *The Village Voice*.
Copyright © 1976 by the Village Voice.

Excerpt from 'The Battle of Aspen' by Hunter S. Thompson,
Copyright © 1970 by Hunter S. Thompson; originally published
in *Rolling Stone* magazine. Used by permission of the author.

Lyrics from "OL '55" by Tom Waits. Copyright © 1972 and 1975
Fifth Floor Music, Inc.

The author also acknowleges with gratitude and appreciation
the *Aspen Times*, 1881–1980, and the files, papers and exhibits of
the Aspen Historical Society. Together, they comprise an
invaluable record and resource. But while the facts in this book
come from those files, the opinions and interpretations of those
facts are those of the author.

Library of Congress Cataloging in Publication Data

Clifford, Peggy.
To Aspen and back.

1. Aspen, Colo.—History. 2. Tourist trade—
Colorado—Aspen—History. I. Title.
F784.A7C56   978.8′43   80–14224
ISBN 0–312–80629–9

The Old West had been settled by dreamers, great hearted adventurers who were unpractical to the point of magnificence, a courteous brotherhood, strong in attack, but weak in defense, who could conquer, but not hold.

Willa Cather

In October 1978 Nina Atwater, an old friend who is never very far from the heart of things, suggested that I finish this book in Philadelphia. The change of scene, the fresh perspective might be helpful, she said. She was right. For twenty-five years, I looked at Aspen. In 1979, at the house of the Atwaters, in Philadelphia, I finally saw Aspen. For that reason, this book is dedicated to Nina Atwater and her daughters, Liz, Rosie and Aubrey. They are bright, generous, funny ladies, and they do not generalize.

PC

CONTENTS

FOREWORD

ASPEN, COLORADO, elevation 7,900 feet, population 6,000. Founded in 1879 by a group of prospectors, site of the richest silver mine in the world and a mother vein forty miles wide. A city of 11,000 by the early 1890s, ruined by the demonetization of silver in 1893. A village of 700 people by 1930, resurrected by a Chicago industrialist in 1945. Site of the Goethe Bicentennial Convocation in 1949, site of the Aspen Music Festival and School and the Aspen Institute for Humanistic Studies, America's largest ski resort. Variously described in recent years as "a town without pity," "the cocaine capital of America," "a candy-ass town," and "THE place of the seventies." Home of leading pop singer John Denver, leading outlaw journalist Hunter S. Thompson, leading best-selling novelist Leon Uris, leading comedian Steve Martin, leading man Jack Nicholson. Playground of Henry Kissinger, Farah, the Shahbanov (the wife of the former Shah of Iran), the Kennedy family, and Cher.

Nothing began in Aspen. Nothing there now is unique —not the mountains, not the summer concerts, not the deep winter snows, not the amiable climate, not the handsome people one sees on the streets, not the drugs that are said to be easy to find there, not the plethora of boutiques and exotic restaurants, not even the astronomical price of real estate. Yet Aspen has entered the national vocabulary.

The Dodge "Aspen" was the "biggest sales success in Dodge history." Two million people bought, and perhaps read, a paperback novel called *Aspen*; upwards of 70 million people watched all or part of an NBC-TV mini-series, "Aspen," based loosely on the book; and an apple-flavored soft drink called Aspen is now available in your supermarket.

More Americans do not care about Aspen than do, of course, but the so-called shapers and movers, the influential, the rich, the famous, the people who chat with Johnny Carson speak of Aspen. Young people in this country, high school and college students, young professionals, young hipsters look on Aspen with a certain awe, believe in it.

Such accomplishments are less original than they are gaudy, bespeak more style than substance, and are not the usual stuff of legends.

It's just a resort, for God's sake. It's beautiful and it's fun, and you can't find better skiing anywhere in America. The concerts are first-rate, and a lot of celebrities go there because it really is mellow and no one hassles them. But it's just a resort, right? Wrong.

Aspen's rise and fall and resurrection, its popularity as a ski resort, its eminence as a summer music center, its recent celebrity are all part of its legend. But somehow the sum is greater than these parts. There is something more, something else. There are no cars named "Martha's Vineyard," no songs in the top forty celebrating the Hamptons, no soft drink called Taos, and there is no town quite like Aspen. It has moved off the travel page and onto the front page. The shapers and movers, the people who name cars and soft drinks and manufacture paperback best sellers are not gamblers. They always opt for the surest thing. Before it was a car or soft drink or best-selling paperback, Aspen was a sure thing.

It does not happen accidentally, this elevation of a place or person to an almost mythic level. There are no accidents. There are only actions and reactions, causes and effects. But it does not happen by design either. No place can put itself on the map unless the map is ready for it.

The relationship between America and Aspen has always been rough and passionate in the way that illicit love affairs are. America made Aspen when it doubled its silver purchases. Three years later the country stopped buying silver and broke Aspen; forgot it and left it up there in the high country to fend for itself. In the postwar years, when America was offering everyone more money and goods than ever before, Aspen turned its back, elevating art and sport over money and goods. In the 1950s, when America was taken very seriously in most places, Aspen mocked it. In the 1960s Aspen turned around and looked America in the eye, saw a big backward place coming late to culture, concern for the environment, the cutting edge of things, and said, "Anything you can do, we can do better." In the 1970s, after years of being out in the cold, out of step, behind America, then ahead of it, then off to one side, the smartass in the mountains was not only accepted but embraced, celebrated.

There is no shortage of civic pride in Aspen and never has been. Most residents will tell you that it is quite simply the only civilized place in America; and the shapers and movers and affluent and young who flock to it in larger and larger numbers agree.

None of this would matter much in a vacuum, but the places we elevate, like the people we elevate, tell us something about ourselves. We tend to think that our heroes are unique, when in fact, they are absolute reflections of us at any given time in history. One can get a very vivid picture of America by simply looking at its heroes, from Thomas Jefferson to John Travolta. Our capitals also reflect us in an absolute way. Since we do not choose heroes or capitals by accident, and since they cannot be consciously made, how and why they emerge matter.

The rise and fall of such phenomena as Perrier water, Studio 54, Farrah Fawcett, *Apocalypse Now,* "Saturday Night Live" and *Rolling Stone* tells us something about ourselves and America, but the elevation of Aspen, a place with a history and a meaning, tells us more. Not everything by any means, but a lot. In the how and why of Aspen's current superstardom, we can see something of ourselves here and now. If you are looking for America, Aspen is not a bad place to start.

I FIRST CAME to Aspen in 1960. I passed through several times and then one time I got stuck. I never intended to live here, and I still don't know why I do, except that I haven't found a better place yet. Actually, I don't live in Aspen. I've always made a point of not living in Aspen. I live in Woody Creek, fifteen miles from Aspen, which used to be a long way. Now it's closer, maybe too close. I view Aspen as some sort of experimental behavioral tank over the mountain.

But for a while I was very much involved in Aspen. It was different then, and the illusions we had about it were different, too. They were not the usual illusions. Aspen has always attracted people who think they can do whatever they want to do. The first post-World War II immigrants to Aspen were skiers from the Army's Tenth Mountain Division. They'd been stationed in Leadville, Colorado, were sent to Italy to fight, and came back to Aspen to live. There wasn't much there, but they were freaks. They didn't care about anything but skiing. Later, most of them turned into fascists.

For a while, Aspen people were so intent on doing their own thing that they didn't have time to bother other people. Now it's full of liberals. The psychic privacy we used to have is gone. There are people here now who are paid to bother other people. That's what Peggy Clifford writes about. She's described the rise and fall of our illusions as well as anyone could. She was right in the middle of it and what she writes is true. She was personally, emotionally and intellectually involved. It was a very high stakes game for her. And for me. Maybe for all of us.

Those old soldiers became rich merchants and they didn't want dirty hippies moving into Aspen and frightening away the big spenders. They began busting people in the streets. I'd come to Aspen to escape politics. Berkeley in the mid-'60s and my long, strange ride with the Hell's Angels had burned me out. But in the summers of 1967 and 1968 in Aspen, it was open season on hippies. My reaction was immediate, highly personal rage. I didn't want those bastards after me. I didn't want to be fined $300 for blocking the sidewalk. Peggy's reaction was more intellectual. She wasn't personally threatened. They weren't coming into her house with search warrants. She and I agreed that the bastards had gone too far and we decided to do something about it. She was idealistic. I was more pragmatic. I tend to be pragmatic about politics. They were after me, I thought. If they could bust one person on the street, they could bust me in my house. And that's how Peggy and I got involved in electing politicians. We did it over and over again. We won all the battles, but I think we lost the war.

There was never a time when I couldn't call Peggy at any hour of the day or night. She was not only here, she was in the middle of it. She was on the streets and every week she'd write about zoning or greedheads or who was lying and who wasn't. She was the intellectual conscience of the town, she was in the trenches and usually in the minority.

A lot of people were afraid of her. She says exactly what she thinks. She is an idealistic and very elegant lady who came out here and bought a bookstore and tried to live her life in as high a way and in as high a place as she could, but she fought the wars, too. She fought an honorable and intelligent battle.

Politics was very close to the bone in Aspen then. You could see it working and you could be a part of it. You could act, say wait a minute, I don't like that, and pick up the telephone and change things by threatening the mayor with a lawsuit or a beating, which we did sometimes. We got more active, running campaigns. Then I ran for sheriff. We elected everyone we wanted to elect except me. We mastered all the techniques. We just never found the solution.

Peggy had worked as hard on my campaign as I had, maybe harder, but she told me one night that she hoped I wouldn't be elected, she hoped I'd lose. I knew she was right. Everyone else was saying hot damn, man, you're going to be sheriff. But she told me what a friend would tell you. It didn't change my mind. I was hoping I wouldn't win either. I was scared to death, but I couldn't say that to anyone, and Peggy was the only person who would say it to me.

Her view here is baleful. She's disillusioned. I feel about Aspen and politics and what we did the way I feel about the peacock eggs in the incubator on my porch. It was a useless expense and I knew the eggs wouldn't hatch, but I felt it was something I had to do. I finally pulled the plug on them after ninety-nine days. I don't feel a sense of failure when I look at the eggs. I did everything I could and they didn't hatch.

I didn't get into politics to be elected to anything, I got in as a dark backroom sinister influence. I thought of it as the politics of enlightened self-interest. If I'm going to live in a place, I don't want some kind of geek running it. And if I have to go head-to-head with the bastards, I will. Peggy really thought we could do it. I thought they were going to come after me and kill me if I won.

The thing that astounded me when I first saw Aspen was that we had so much room here, more room than I'd ever seen anywhere. It was the best of all possible worlds. The skiers brought free enterprise and Walter Paepcke brought the aesthetics. It was the perfect mix. You could dance to the music of your own cash register and then go off to a concert while your daughter sat on a rock in the river listening to a famous painter talk about art. But Paepcke's ideal was impossible to live up to. He erected a set of pretensions that have overshadowed the town ever since. I saw politics as an act of self-defense. They were after me and they were going to take the meadow in front of my house and change it unless I fought with them. Like everyone else who's survived, I know that if you turn your back on the bastards, they'll cut you down.

The greedheads work eight days a week. The trouble is that the greedheads, the real estate developers and the people who want to buy and sell quick and move on work harder than I do. I'm a writer. I'm a lazy person. Peggy's that way, too. We can't work eight days a week and fight those bastards. We don't get paid for it. They do. It's in their interest to grind up the valley and sell it for gravel, but it is not in my interest. They're merchants. I've never made a fucking nickel off this valley, and neither has Peggy. We were here for different reasons.

Peggy's moved to Philadelphia. I think she felt it was time for her to move on, but she also got caught in the economic crunch. I could be next. I have 122 acres. I have a fortress, but it could be taken away from me through zoning or taxes, by an act of politicians, politicians I elected. These monsters are zoning me out of existence now. Still winning the battle, still losing the war.

We had the idea that you should be able to live the way you wanted to and in the highest way you could imagine, but some people wanted to keep it the way it was and some people wanted to grind it up and sell it for gravel. There was always a degree of madness in what we did. We used radio then the way politicians use television now. Nobody had ever used the radio politically before in Aspen. We scared the piss out of people. Peggy wrote some of the best ads I've ever seen in any political campaign. Massive, long, intelligent political screeds. She doesn't talk about that much here. She alludes to it. She uses "we" a lot. But she was involved seven nights a week, sometimes all night.

I don't much like politics here anymore. Now you fight unknown persons, human X factors, computer programmers. But I can still sit here and see the mountains with the sun coming up over them because when it was necessary we went out and made enemies and worked *nine* days a week. We did that. God didn't do that, or the est-ers. By the end of the sixties, Aspen had become a valley of idle rich, a valley of victims. It's prey to any kind of bullshit now. It's a monument to the relentless masochism of the idle rich. Maybe the party's over here now, but the cops didn't break it up, the people did. As the new money poured in, the party began to get rancid. For Werner Erhard, and the other new gurus, it was like shooting fish in a barrel. But the ethic of everything's okay, we're all okay and everything's perfect, just didn't mix with the fuck you, get off my land and don't put the God damn highway down here, we don't like it ethic. It's passive as opposed to active. The activist ethic was overwhelmed. The sharp edge that we'd brought to it went dull.

There are many pillars of salt along the highway now. The highway from Aspen is Glenwood Springs is lined with pillars of salt. It was an individual utopia, now it's a corporate utopia. Peggy's talking about that, I think.

As a writer, what I appreciate most in this book is the clarity and validity of Peggy's descriptions of people and times and places. You almost had to be there to know how good the writing is. She was always the chronicler of reality in town. When she was doing the column, she knew what was happening and she knows what's happening now. She ties Aspen's fate to America. She knows what's happening in America, too. But as a politician, a combatant, what interests me is that she concluded that all our best efforts in politics came to nothing. Sometimes, I believe that. I believed that when I finished the book.

One of my most intense memories of Peggy goes back to the night Bobby Kennedy was shot, and tonight Vernon Jordan was shot. Twelve years later, almost to the day. It never ends, the bastards never sleep. Vernon Jordan, head of one of the most conservative black organizations, is shot in Fort Wayne, Indiana, and Ronald Reagan is going to be our next president. In that context, you can't say Aspen has failed. I look out here and see the same mountains and the same fields I've seen for ten years. I had to fight savagely to protect them, but they're still there, no matter how precarious my hold on them is, so maybe we haven't failed. But you sure as hell can't say we've succeeded. Of course, you can't create a valley for the rich and then expect to live in peace with them. The rich are monsters.

This book was not an assignment, not some scholarly treatise. It is an act of passion. Peggy was in the trenches. She's the ultimate authority. She wrote one of the most intelligent columns in the history of American journalism. Her collected columns on Aspen would be a real saga, a million words or more. No one did what she did. Nobody else wrote with the consistency, the genuine love for the valley that she did. Other people might have felt it, but she said it. Other people wrote gossip columns. And she wasn't sitting in some upstairs window at the Aspen Historical Society watching it from a distance, she was right down there in the thick of it.

On a Wednesday night in November, 1960, it was snowing, and I showed up on Peggy's doorstep. A total stranger, a freak from Kentucky with a pile of trash on top of a car that had to be delivered to some decorator in Aspen. I thought Peggy would be horrified. I had no place to go, no money, and I couldn't even leave town until I got the money from the decorator. Peggy fed me, gave me a place to sleep, money for the train when the decorator quibbled, and a ride to the train in Glenwood Springs. Here came a vagrant through town, a Neal Cassady kind of freak, traveling with a giant doberman and a monster dog crate that was heavy and made to be a home for the dog on the train, if we ever got on the train, and she took care of everything.

If she ran a salon, as people said, first in her bookstore, later in her house, that's the kind of salon she ran, a refuge for the right people, meaning, in most people's eyes, the wrong people. She was and is a very discriminating lady.

Hunter S. Thompson
Woody Creek, Colorado
May 29, 1980

Through the Looking Glass

I FIRST HEARD of Aspen in 1949 when a professor of mine told me of old mountains, graceful streams, breakfasts with Albert Schweitzer, drinks with Gary Cooper. I doubted the existence of such a place, but I wanted to believe him and I did. Film stars and geniuses. It was all I wanted.

I didn't go there immediately. I was utterly caught up in my vagrant life in the big old eastern cities and their outposts. I spent a winter in Pittsburgh, part of a summer on a Delaware beach and the rest of the time bucketing from rich times in Greenwich and on New York's smart East Side to poor times in Yonkers and Greenwich Village. But one by one, my friends in New York buttoned up and settled down. They were going to have careers and families; I was determined to have a life.

In June 1953, I headed west, traveling by train because I had the notion in those days that one truly saw America on a train, that there one met truly interesting people who, being in transit and temporarily cut off from the mundane facts of things, were capable of astounding insights. Besides, I loved the taste of vanilla ice cream on those rough, heavy, slightly yellow imitation silver spoons that were to be found only in the dining rooms of exclusive clubs and on trains.

I didn't see America because I got bored looking out of the window about six hours into my journey. I didn't encounter any interesting people—only grubby young soldiers and seriously overweight people with faces like oatmeal, and squally children, and gray old people with the temperaments of stones. I ate a lot of vanilla ice cream, however, and hung around late at night in the club car, flirting cautiously with soldiers and pretending I was a journalist on a major story, hurtling through the night after Truth, the answers to the Big Questions.

I felt myself superior to America. The country had been heroic during the war but gone timid and lifeless afterward, as if it had used itself all up. Harry Truman had ended the war abruptly by dropping the Big Bomb on Hiroshima. The United Nations was organized with the aim of preventing further wars, but England's Prime Minister, Winston Churchill, spoke of the "Iron Curtain" that separated us from our recent ally, the Soviet Union. We dropped test bombs in the Pacific as peace treaties were being signed. Americans were horrified when, during the Nuremberg trials of Nazi leaders, the stories of the Holocaust emerged. We heard of millions of Jews being wiped out in the most hideous ways, and yet anti-Semitism flourished here. Planes were flying at supersonic speeds, the transistor was invented at Bell Labs, and Thor Heyerdahl sailed on a raft from Peru to Polynesia in 101 days to prove his theory of prehistoric migration. Congress passed the Marshall Plan Act, sending $17 billion in aid to Europe, and rocket missiles were tested in New Mexico. China became a Communist power, American soldiers went to Korea, and Senator

Joe McCarthy was busily unraveling our Bill of Rights as
he hunted for Communists in our government. We
seemed to be opposing and aping totalitarianism simultaneously. The clearly unconstitutional McCarran-Nixon
Internal Security Act, the execution of the Rosenbergs as
spies, the testing of a bigger bomb, the witch hunt in
Hollywood for Communists, the continuing popularity
of McCarthy—all seemed profoundly un-American to
me.

In 1952 Dwight D. Eisenhower and Adlai Stevenson
were the Presidential candidates. Eisenhower was a Republican, a professional soldier, Supreme Commander in
Europe during World War II, a folksy inarticulate golfer.
Stevenson was a Democrat, a lawyer, former governor of
Illinois, an aristocrat with enormous compassion for poor
people. I admired aristocrats and poor people, and didn't
much like anyone else. I didn't know many poor people,
but I had read about them and often saw them from the
train when I went through Harlem on my way to Greenwich. Stevenson was intelligent, witty and critical of the
state of the Union. I liked what he said and I liked the
way he said it. I worked on his campaign, writing pithy
sound-truck pitches. He lost. I wanted no part of America after that, and since I had neither the means nor the
wiles to get to Europe that summer, I headed for Aspen.
It was, I had convinced myself, an anomaly, the final
outpost of freedom and originality in a gray-flannel nation.

Denver was my first stop, and it was discouraging, the
most pitiful city I'd ever seen. It was like a small town
that didn't know it was a small town and kept adding
onto itself. It seemed to exemplify that terminal Bab-
bittry, that celebration of middle-class materialism I so

despised in postwar America. Its buildings seemed new
and unsubstantial, its people homely and eager, its
streets hectic and sleazy. It was cleaner than New York,
but hungrier. The Brown Palace Hotel was more encouraging. Built during the silver boom in the 1890s, it
was elegant in a grandiose sort of way, and no one there
said "ain't."

I met some Aspen people for lunch at the Brown and
sat next to Fred Glidden, a novelist who wrote westerns
under the name of Luke Short. Yes, I said to myself, this
is it. Here I am, having martinis with a famous and successful writer. I would have preferred Faulkner or some
other novelist I had previously heard of, but I liked Glidden immediately. He wore thick horn-rimmed glasses, a
tweed jacket, gray flannels, and was a man of mild demeanor, good humor and profound melancholy. During
lunch, he talked well and truly about American writers
and his disappointment in his own work. His books were,
he said, trite, trivial and unworthy. They pay the bills, he
said, that's all. Though I had never read any of his books,
I protested. Geniuses were always dissatisfied with their
own work. I said the western was an indigenous American art form, like jazz. He changed the subject.

You will like Aspen, he said. It is a fine quirky place.
There are people there who are straight out of Fitz-
gerald, he said, golden people whose appetites are as
extraordinary as their charms. They do nothing in the
ordinary way. They play hard and work hard and have
no conventional ambitions. They love neither wisely nor
well, but abundantly. Aspen, I concluded, was plainly
Greenwich and Greenwich Village put magically together in the mountains—the best of all possible worlds.

After lunch, my traveling companions loaded my gear

into their car and we headed west out of Denver. The
Rockies rising out of the plains are one of the world's
truly astonishing sights. There is no preface, no warning.
The plains simply end and the mountains begin, and
moving from one to the other is like moving from one
planet to another. As we came into the mountains, I felt
as if I were returning to the beginning, before man,
before time, before anything was present but stone and
seed. Until that moment I had hardly been aware of the
natural world, but suddenly it was the entire world. We
moved up and up until we had left trees and grass behind. The car engine whined a little. The air was thin
and cool. When we reached the top of Loveland Pass on
the Continental Divide, I took one last look back. From
that height, it seemed already vague, abstract, like some
premise that hadn't quite worked out.

We drove down the western slope of the Divide
through forests that were still cold though it was June,
shot through a marshy, grassy plain and into Glenwood
Canyon. Formed by the Colorado River several mil-
lennia ago, its red-stone walls, intricate and very tall,
rose straight up from the slow, slow river.

This was the American frontier, I thought—still open,
endless and untamed. It was the West. Not the silly card-
board West that I'd seen in movies, but the real West
that men had never breached—rugged, vast and original. Anything was possible here. Men and women, if they
were rugged and original too, could live here in another
way. Fred Glidden said there were such people in
Aspen.

Beyond the canyon, the Roaring Fork River enters the
Colorado. We crossed over a long bridge into Glenwood
Springs, at the mouth of the Roaring Fork Valley. I never

saw a town that tried so hard to be ordinary, to resist the grand promise of the West. It had stoplights, men's oxfords in store windows, garden hoes and trowels on display in front of a hardware store, ranks of recapped white-wall tires at a gas station. I saw women in housedresses carrying bags of groceries, men in suits and ties carrying plastic briefcases. It was Main Street, America, set down in the middle of this vast wilderness.

Fifteen miles up the valley, we passed Carbondale, a flat pastoral town that was at least a generation behind Glenwood. A fine mist hung over green sultry meadows. Mount Sopris, the perfect movie mountain, rose up beyond Carbondale like a great symmetrical sentinel in the valley. On up the road, we sped by Basalt, a tiny tilted town that spelled out its name in large white rocks on a hillside and seemed to go in for grain and other farm supplies. It was located even further back in time than Carbondale. Beyond Basalt, there were thick stands of spruce, cottonwood and aspen trees, acres of wildflowers, old log farmhouses, tilting barns, pastures with rough rail fences strung with sagging barbed wire, and the river showing us the way.

The Roaring Fork River begins at the top of the Continental Divide and gathers speed and size as it rolls forty-two miles down to the Colorado River. Fed by Hunter, Castle, Maroon, Woody and Snowmass creeks, and the Frying Pan and Crystal rivers, it is the maker and master of the valley. Absolutely faithful to the river's course, the valley is shallow and broad in some places, pinched high and tight in other places.

Seventy-five years before, the long graceful valley was part of the Ute Indians' territory. They called the river that made the valley Thunder. Ferdinand Hayden's

Atlas of Colorado, published in the 1870s, showed that 3,500 Utes lived in the Central Rockies. It also showed rich mineral formations at the head of the Thunder River. In June 1879, a group of prospectors struggled over the Rockies from Leadville, a booming silver camp, and pitched their tents in the high meadow at the head of the valley. The Utes were not present. There were few signs of their habitation. They did not come back. It is said that when the Utes left the valley for the last time, they placed a curse on it: "The white man will never prosper off this land as long as the grass grows and the water flows."

In the Thunder River Valley, as elsewhere in the West, what the government gave back to the Indians was usually taken away by the government itself or by advancing legions of pioneers. The men who crossed the Divide cared nothing for federal compacts. They'd seen men like themselves become millionaires in Leadville. They were ambitious and single-minded, and the signs of silver were infinitely more compelling than vague policies made in Washington.

ASPEN WAS, at first sight, as wonderful and mysterious as the mountains. Main Street, long, straight and wide, was lined with tall cottonwood trees that were as large around as barrels at their bases and feathery at their tops. Shaggy mountains rose on both sides of the town, but it was spacious and airy and, aside from certain beaches in the early morning, the most encouraging landscape I'd ever seen. There were no signs of what Chambers of Commerce call "progress"—no neon signs, no bright lights, no commotion. It was not that Aspen lagged behind the times, as Carbondale and Basalt had; it was somehow out of time. Aspen hadn't renounced progress. It had just forgot it, in the way that dogs who get lost in the wilderness forget they are pets.

I had plainly come to a pause in the world. In 1953 Aspen was a town that had once been a city, a boom town, a silver capital that had been stripped back to its bones by time and circumstance. The prospectors had found silver, millions of dollars worth of it, and dug it and sold it, but in 1893 Washington said it had enough silver. Rich men became paupers, poor men just left. For a while money was in the air like sun. There in that remote valley the American Dream had taken root, flowered and bloomed silver, and there too it had withered and died. I recalled the Ute curse: "The white man will never prosper off this land as long as the grass grows and the water flows."

Aspen had been made in the 1880s and 1890s for comfort, growth, movement, and then it had been remade for survival. Everything that was not vital had been jettisoned during its long decades of decline, in the way that pilots jettison unnecessary weight when their engines go. After years in elaborate complicated cities, I found Aspen amazing, and in some fundamental way, consoling. A skeleton is, after all, more comprehensible than an entire body, and bones are almost always handsomer than flesh.

In 1953 Aspen was made as much of space as of stuff. In downtown Aspen, as in its neighborhoods, there were few buildings. Many had burned down, had been torn down or had simply fallen down. Each building was separate, distinct, a monument to its own staying power. The entire town was very low to the ground; the largest buildings were the Hotel Jerome, the Wheeler Opera

House, the Elks Building and the city hall. Any one of them would have fit comfortably into the lobby of an ordinary New York skyscraper. They had been built in the 1890s by men who thought they owned the world. As it turned out, the men were wrong, but the buildings endured and became crucial facts in the townscape, imposing a certain order and scale, suggesting that character matters more than money or power or anything.

In Aspen's neighborhoods, there were more one-story houses than two-story houses, more small houses than large, and even the largest were not very elaborate. In the late afternoon, the cottonwood trees cast long shadows across wide yards and vacant lots. Fragile and full of light, the aspen trees were in constant motion. There were no sidewalks, but there were irrigation ditches in which clear cold water ran. On some afternoons, the sky literally fell down and drenched everything, but an hour later the streets were dusty again. There were no paved streets except Main Street, which was part of State Highway 82.

DOWNTOWN ASPEN measured no more than three blocks by four blocks. People came and went from stores and shops, bought and sold, but commerce seemed a sideline rather than the main thing. I was drawn to Tomkins Hardware, a store as quiet and solemn as a library. In its bins of rough-cut wood were more nails in more shapes than one could imagine. Implements hung from the ceiling, hoes and shovels and wire cutters and saws made of gray-blue metal and hard yellow wood. It was always dim and cool. Its upper shelves were nearly empty. A tall white-haired man in a clean faded denim apron presided there, Tomkins himself. It seemed an authentic remnant from some sweeter time in America. It was as significant to me as the Museum of Modern Art had been. There was Truth in both places, but it was more accessible here, I thought. Schweitzer had gone back to Africa, Gary Cooper had gone back to Hollywood, but Mr. Tomkins was still here, and so was Truth.

1⌃
How It Came to Be

THE FREE, open and endless frontier was and is our most popular legend. Editorial writers said, "Go west, young men," and the young men did. Adventurers, outcasts, immigrants, misfits, paupers, rebels, rogues, fanatics, farmers, prospectors, once and future barons: they fought blizzards, drought, each other, faced extraordinary hardships, and they prevailed. But their deeds, heroic and shameful, reside always in the shadow of the idea of the frontier.

Every place has some dominant quality that sets its tone and temper. I'm not sure how such a quality evolves, or what its source is, but I know that every town and city has one, perhaps even before it's a town or a city. It may just be there, like weather, vegetation, longitude and latitude, topography, or it may emerge from those things. Or it may be part of the birthing, arriving with the reason for the place. From 1879 to the present, the dominant quality, the axis on which everything else in Aspen has turned, has been hubris, that presumptuous sense of self-importance that resides in big-time crooks and geniuses. It goes hand-in-hand with the idea of the free, open and endless frontier, instructs us that we not only can have everything, but that we deserve it. Hubris

11

is a peculiarly American quality, and nowhere in America has it flourished longer or more openly than it has in Aspen.

As much as anything else, hubris drove the first prospectors over the untracked mountains into Indian territory. It sent men down into the mountains' steep recesses to mine millions of dollars worth of silver. It inspired these same men and others to make not just a camp, but a handsome and sturdy town in that high and wild place. The first wagon to reach Aspen was carried in piece by piece by prospectors and reassembled on arrival. In 1881 Aspen had only thirty-five residents, but the Colorado State Assembly carved 950 square miles out of Gunnison County to the south and named the new county Pitkin after Governor Frederick Pitkin. The camp had been named Ute City, but as no one had any interest in commemorating the first residents of the valley, or even remembering them, the town was called Aspen.

By 1884 Aspen claimed a population of 2,500, fifteen stores, seven saloons, three hotels and a daily newspaper. In 1885 it became the state's first "all-electric city," beating out Denver and other larger cities. It now boasted ten churches, three banks, six newspapers, an imposing red sandstone courthouse, an armory, a city hall, a hospital and the Pitkin County Jockey Club's 200-acre racetrack. One journalist wrote that Aspen was "the handsomest and most substantial town in the Rockies." *Harper's Weekly* commended Aspen for its "unyielding respectability and force of character," ignorant perhaps of the "soiled doves" who worked out of cribs and houses near the Colorado Midland Depot at the bottom of Aspen Mountain, and of the brutal battles that went on in the mines.

Nothing in the valley had the force and respectability of silver. In January 1880 Henry Gillespie and a partner bought a mining claim for $1,000. By the middle of the decade, it was sold for $600,000. Gillespie's Molly Gibson Consolidated Mining Company—which spread across sixty-four acres—was the richest silver mine in the world. Between 1880 and 1893, $105 million in silver was taken out of Aspen's mountains. But the town was blessed in other ways, too.

On the high plains east of the Rockies, there was a terrible and endless flatness on which, after years, towns still rode uncertainly. But long before the Aspen townsite was stepped out, the Roaring Fork Valley was wholly habitable. Valley farms produced excellent hay and a variety of grains, vegetables and fruits. Water, the most valuable resource of all in the arid West, was abundant. Thick stands of yellow pine provided plenty of lumber for the booming town. Ranchers raised sheep and cattle. Independence, several miles east of Aspen, became a leading gold camp. Ashcroft, southwest of Aspen, was producing silver too.

In 1881 the *Aspen Times* rhapsodized, "The mines of this county are all tributary to Independence, Aspen and Ashcroft, and in contemplating their wealth, who can venture to foretell their future or to predict with any degree of certainty the numbers of the vast population destined to inhabit Pitkin County? Soon the shrill whistle of the smelter will wake the echoes in the valley of the Roaring Fork and the hurry and bustle of a metropolis will be upon us. . . . in their season will come the tourist and invalid seeking the rest and recuperation which only a beautiful and life-giving climate can bestow."

In 1893, however, the *Times*'s tune changed. "The Money of the Constitution is dishonored, slaughtered in the land of its friends, and the curtain fell with loud applause from the goldbug gallery. British bouquets in great profusion lie at the feet of Grover, the chief actor in the conspiracy, and he does not hear the wail of distress and suffering that comes up from the people."

In 1890 Congress had passed the Sherman Silver Purchase Act, requiring the Treasury to nearly double its silver purchases and radically increase the amount of money in circulation. This, however, threatened to undermine the Treasury's gold reserves. In the wake of the panic of 1893, President Grover Cleveland called Congress into special session to repeal the Sherman Act and demonetize silver. As word reached Colorado of Cleveland's call, silver prices began to drop. Within a few months, 30,000 men were out of work in the state. On November 4, 1893, the Sherman Act was repealed and Aspen was on the skids.

During Aspen's first fourteen years many divergent impulses were demonstrated. It was a mining camp, but it was not like other mining camps. When its first residents were still living in tents, they began a Sunday school and a literary society. It was a western town, but it was not like other western towns. Its topography, climate and abundant natural resources made it seem a kind of cradle or fort, depending on the drift of one's imagination. It bore a resemblance to those solid Nebraska towns described by Willa Cather, but only a superficial resemblance. Its grid had a traditional logic, expressed traditional notions of the city, but its houses, public buildings and pleasures were freewheeling, sophisticated, fashionable.

Aspen's first residents were stubborn ambitious people, willing and able to put up with any hardship to get their way; when they hit paydirt, they immediately began living up to or beyond their means. They were incapable of imagining the end of the boom, or of accepting it when it came. For decades after the demonetization of silver, hope rang in the Roaring Fork Valley like a bell. Surely Washington would come to its senses. Surely the price of silver would rise. Surely there was a future in tourism. Again and again the *Aspen Times* proclaimed NEW ERA ABOUT TO BEGIN. Hubris prepares one only for success.

Other mining towns, including both Independence and Ashcroft, withered into uselessness or died. Aspen went on believing in itself—as both fact and promise. The hubris that brought the first prospectors to Aspen, that drove them into the depths of the mountains and compelled them to make a city in the wilderness remained intact. They had wandered and stopped and made a town. They had dug silver and made a fortune. When there were no more buyers, they waited. According to the *Aspen Times,* the requisite philosophy was "smile and push," and the goal was to put "Aspen back on the map." While there seemed to be some smiling and pushing, little tangible effort was made to improve Aspen's economy.

The Crystal City Boosters Association began to lobby for the construction of a national highway between Aspen and Twin Lakes on the eastern slope, so that all those travelers who surely wanted to come to Aspen could get there easily. The road was not built and the travelers did not come. Women's civic groups raised money for a national advertising program to promote the valley as a sportsmen's paradise, but nothing came of their efforts either. Virtually all of the elk in the valley had been shot by miners and railroad crews, so twenty-one elk were imported from Idaho to build a new herd that would surely attract hunters. But it didn't. The Trocadero, "Aspen's newest dancing resort," opened. It offered "good healthy amusement" with its $1,700 "Wurlitzer full-orchestra piano." Early in 1926 the *Times* announced: ASPEN IS ASSURED OF A PERIOD OF UNEQUALLED PROSPERITY. In March 1926 the Aspen Smelting Company closed. In October 1926 silver prices dropped to a new low of 26 cents an ounce. By the end of the year, the daily *Times* had become a weekly. In 1930 Aspen's population was 705, and though the Depression had turned the nation in a different direction, Aspen went on waiting.

The American belief in the happy ending is a source of endless entertainment for the rest of the world, but it is that belief that is the basis for America's unequalled accomplishments—its growth, its prosperity, its power. In the world lexicon, failure is bound to follow success. In the American lexicon, success is bound to follow failure too. Everything has aspects of the phoenix. There are always new bets to make, new rainbows to follow, new pots of gold to seek. There is something fundamentally consoling about the process. In America the dentist becomes the gunman, the gunman becomes the sheriff, the madam becomes the mayor, the boom town becomes the ghost town, the silver camp becomes a rich and handsome town. Nothing is forever, except hubris.

2 ∧
Thinking Small,
Dreaming Big

J EROME B. WHEELER, the president of Macy's in New York, came to Colorado to take the waters at Manitou Springs and stayed to ride the boom in Aspen. He bought the partially completed Castle Creek smelter, a number of mining claims and some coal mines. He founded a banking house, was a large stockholder in the Colorado Midland Railroad and, with the profits from all of that, built the Wheeler Opera House and the Hotel Jerome.

The opera house had, in its day, featured such acts as a champion lady fencer, the Schubert Quintette of Chicago, which consisted of four male singers and a harp, and Conreid's English Opera Company "under the personal direction of Heinrich Conreid." A Paris chef concocted delicacies in the Jerome kitchen as Wheeler's miners undertook less civilized chores. When he sent his men to seize a mine shaft that another man had claimed, they were hit with blasts of sulphurous steam. In 1893 Wheeler's empire collapsed. The opera house stage went dark and was subsequently destroyed by fire. The building itself, made of heavy stone blocks, survived.

The Jerome lobby has always been the center of Aspen. In 1953 residents came and went in what was then the uniform—Levi's or Bermuda shorts, Brooks

Brothers shirts and Topsiders. They were tan easy people, careless in both senses of the word, jokers. The hotel guests were somewhat paler, softer, rounder. They dressed in what were called "leisure clothes," and looked to me as if they might be from the lesser suburbs of major cities. Self-made and sincere, they lingered in the lobby, endlessly grouping and regrouping. There was an eagerness about them that suggested they believed all the Big Questions had answers and that there were people who knew more than they did. The residents were not so humble.

If the Jerome lobby was the center of Aspen, Walter P. Paepcke held the center. It was not possible to be in Aspen for more than a day in 1953 without hearing of Paepcke. He was, I had been told, the maker of modern Aspen and its king. His wife Elizabeth had come to Aspen in 1939 on a lark. It was as dead and poor as a town can be, but she fell in love with it. In the spring of 1945, she brought her husband to see it. He saw what she had seen and saw something more.

From the beginning, people had known that there was more in the valley than silver. In 1880 B. Clark Wheeler, lecturing around the West, described Aspen as "a paradise for sportsmen and artists." In 1911 Jack Leahy, a leading citizen, announced that he was going to build "a complete authentic Swiss village" and turn Pitkin County into "the playground of the world." Nothing came of it. In the late 1930s a group of rich young Californians tried to turn the area into a ski resort. They built a sixteen-bed lodge, commissioned the reigning American wit, Robert Benchley, to write a brochure called *How to Aspen,* and imported Swiss ski champion André Roch to advise them. When World War II began in September 1939, one of the young entrepreneurs, Billy

Fiske, went to England and enlisted in the Royal Air Force. He was the first American flyer to be shot down over Europe. His friends abandoned the ski resort plan.

What Paepcke saw that no one else had seen was that Aspen's apparent drawbacks—its remote location and decades of poverty—were actually assets. Its remote location could be seen as exclusiveness and serenity. Its poverty could be seen as purity. Its drawbacks would become the foundation for Aspen's revival.

When he met with townspeople in Pitkin County Courthouse in September 1945, Paepcke noted that the town was moribund economically, lacked essential services, had no doctor, no laundry, no firetrucks. The town's water was bad. There was no sewer system. The people were dispirited. He'd seen drunks sitting in the gutters in broad daylight. But, he went on, the town was unique and beautiful. Nothing had been built there in forty years. It was purely Victorian. His newly formed Aspen Company planned to lease and restore the Hotel Jerome, the opera house and a number of old houses. The Aspen Skiing Corporation, also organized by him, would continue the work that André Roch had begun. Trails would be cut, lifts would be built on Aspen Mountain on the south edge of town. A summer enterprise, the Aspen Institute for Humanistic Studies, would round out and balance the economy.

Paepcke spoke that day of nourishing "the whole man," of challenging him aesthetically and intellectually as well as physically. He himself was more scholar than athlete and had long been a patron of the arts in Chicago, where he was born and lived. Here, he said, in this remote and gorgeous setting far from the urban commotion, valuable work in arts and letters would be done.

The development of Aspen Mountain and the creation

of a summer arts program would, he said, restore Aspen's fortunes and spirit without violating its beauty and character. It would, in fact, complement them. In the rest of America, sport and art were seen as diversions. In Aspen they would be the main things. President Calvin Coolidge had said twenty years before that "the business of America was business." Paepcke seemed to be saying that the business of Aspen would be happiness, in the Jeffersonian sense. Work and play would be fused and would be profitable in tangible and intangible ways.

If there were people present that day who thought the Chicago industrialist was a fool—and I'm sure there were—they did not say it out loud, because it was not only the best offer, it was the only offer they'd had in a long, long time. It was a classic western scenario. The stranger comes to town and changes the town's direction fundamentally. In the movies, no one messes with the stranger, and in Aspen no one messed with Paepcke.

EIGHT YEARS LATER, when I first saw Paepcke, he had already worked his will on the place and was clearly the boss, yet he retained some of the airs of the stranger. He had a lean, swept-back, almost streamlined face. He was unfailingly polite, but his smile came hard and awkwardly. People swirled around him—artists, scholars, big businessmen, politicians—all brought by him to Aspen, all a little uncomfortable in their casual clothes, tugging at imaginary ties, waiting to do his bidding. It was as if he was the only person who knew the whole story and he was telling it very slowly, keeping the best part to himself, relying solely on his own intelligence, his own vision, editing and embellishing as he went along. Walter and Elizabeth Paepcke were in their prime, a handsome couple with more money and brains than most of

their peers. Instead of traveling or buying yachts or col-
lecting art as their peers did, they chose to turn a shattered town into a kind of national treasure of arts and
ideas. It was not an act of philanthropy. It was an act of
passion—and hubris.

Men had restored quaint villages before, had cleared
trails and built lifts on mountains before, and had
erected intellectual monuments to themselves before,
but no one had done what Paepcke had done and no one
had thought of doing anything like it in postwar America.

Having survived the Depression, won the war, and
achieved a new global clout, America was a country from
which nothing could be withheld. Not since its beginnings had it offered such fertile stuff to dreamers. The
land had been assembled, the cities built, the machines
made, the wars fought and won, the economy stabilized.
The horizon was, if anything, wider and more encouraging than it had been in 1775. It was a propitious time for
every sort of odyssey, yet most Americans feared the
Bomb, the Red Menace, and chased after money, things
and something they called "security." They could have
had the moon, but they chose security. For it they were
willing not only to tolerate the bullyboy tactics of such
demagogues as Joe McCarthy, but to toe the line in their
jobs, their neighborhoods and their clubs. No one
wanted to be caught doing anything that everyone else
wasn't doing, or so it seemed. America had gone to war
to preserve life, liberty and the pursuit of happiness, and
had come home to deny life, restrict liberty and pursue
security.

Paepcke and the people who followed him to Aspen
did not want money, things and security. They wanted
something more or something less, it was not entirely

clear then. Almost uniformly upper middle-class, broadly educated, essentially cosmopolitan in outlook, they would not or could not toe the line. Aspen was everything postwar America was not—chaste, untroubled, eager.

It was also well out of America's way. Deep in the mountains, it was a six-hour drive from Denver in good weather, cut off in bad. It had no television, only the feeblest and most erratic radio signals. Newspapers arrived a day late from Denver. Forests rolled back to unimaginable depths, were full of primeval odors. Deer, elk and skunk sported in backyards. Aspen had no paved streets, stoplights, central heating, best sellers, supermarkets, traffic jams, air pollution, crime or juvenile delinquency. But in 1953 it had two bookstores and Aspen shops sold Venini glass, Irish sweaters, Pucci dresses, Gucci leathers and Andy Warhol drawings long before they became status symbols. Only one of the owners of the five leading restaurants had any previous restaurant experience—which, as someone said, explained why the restaurants were so unusual. One served opera with the linguini, and a jazz harpist performed in the Jerome dining room. Croissants rather than hot dogs were the staple items of Aspen menus. Pitkin County Bank would loan money only to people who had no need of loans, but in my first week in Aspen, young, broke and without any visible prospects, I was offered charge accounts at virtually every store I entered. Partially owned by the Paepckes, Aspen Lumber and Supply sold young builders all their materials on credit and was remarkably tolerant of backsliders. Beck and Bishop, the grocery store, did not blink if a customer's bill topped $1,000, as long as he kept coming in.

Paepcke's Aspen seemed to be the only place in the

nation trying to keep the nation's postwar promise alive. But its simplicity, its optimism, its innocence were less spontaneous than they were willed. Events had tossed Aspen out of time. Walter Paepcke was determined to keep it out of time. That, he saw, was its principal asset in rancorous materialistic postwar America.

LIKE THE SONS of many well-to-do families in the early twentieth century, Paepcke had had a classical education, went off to Yale, and came home to take over the family company. In time he built it into the giant Container Corporation of America. He also became a trustee of the University of Chicago, the Chicago Art Institute and the Chicago Orchestral Association. He was one of the first participants in Dr. Mortimer Adler's great books seminars, in which adults gathered together to study classic works. None of that was sufficient for Paepcke. He wanted more, and when he saw Aspen, all that he had learned and all that he had dreamed of coalesced. His scholarly and aesthetic interests told him what to do. His business savvy told him how to do it.

His friend and ally Robert Maynard Hutchins, the chancellor of the University of Chicago, wrote of him, "Although business was fascinating to Walter Paepcke, and he was very good at it, he did not regard an exclusive preoccupation with it as suitable to a civilized man. . . . The development of Aspen was typical. He saw it first as a ghost town worth preserving as such. He then began to think of it as an American Salzburg. Finally, he made it one of the great cultural centers of America. . . ."

MAJOR DECISIONS were made not in the Pitkin County Courthouse or the city hall, but in the Jerome lobby, at the bar or at the pool. The pool was a kind of cross between a country club and a great books seminar. Tall, slender, with the face of a great beauty and the demeanor of a queen, Elizabeth Paepcke moved about the pool as if she were the hostess of a wonderful party that commenced every day at noon. Her parents, Professor and Mrs. William Nitze, were often on hand. The Nitzes were small, very old but very alert and somewhat bemused by the sight of premier labor leader Walter Reuther, premier philosopher Mortimer Adler and premier violist William Primrose, each as pale and plump as the other, sporting in the pool or huddling under a patio umbrella, resolving all the Big Questions. The Nitzes seemed to admire their daughter as much as everyone else did. The Paepckes' three daughters spent their days at the pool too: Paula, the stayer; Nina, the rebel; and Toni, the beauty. Like their father, they stood somewhat apart.

If the royal family had a prime minister, he was Herbert Bayer. An Austrian artist who came to America several years before the war, he met Paepcke when he was commissioned to do a series of ads for the Container Corporation called "The Great Ideas of Western Man." The ads, which combined classic quotations with modern paintings over a discreet CCA logo, were as high-toned as advertising got in those days. Paepcke invited Bayer to move to Aspen and assist him with its resurrection and restoration. Like many of his fellow Bauhaus masters, Bayer worked in all media—architecture, painting, graphics and sculpture—and like them, he was an advocate of clean, even severe, modernism in all things. But he spoke often too of the value of authenticity and aesthetic integrity. He had the face, bearing and slow deep voice of a great actor; and he saw Aspen, all air and bones when he arrived, as a kind of stage on which he could create a masterpiece—everything in harmony, everything pleasing to the eye, everything resolved intellectually along Bauhaus lines.

With Paepcke, he set down guidelines for the townscape that were meant to preserve its small scale and Victorian character. He superintended the restoration of the Aspen Company's old buildings and tried to persuade newcomers to build simple honest modern structures rather than the pseudo-Victorian houses, ersatz Swiss chalets and motel-modern edifices that turned up in other mountain towns. He was not always successful.

His restoration of the opera house was scrupulous. When it was done, the building looked purely Victorian. The miners of 1890 would have felt entirely at home there. But it is impossible to know what they would have thought of the remade Hotel Jerome. Bayer ordered its red bricks painted two shades of grey. The arches over the windows were painted blue—Bayer blue it came to be called. He had made the old building modern, even startling, and some natives thought it was hideous. The blue "eyebrows," they said, made the fine old building a joke. Traditionally, Victorian houses were painted in dark colors with white trim. Bayer used light colors, often three or four on one house. Purists protested. Bayer responded by saying that the use of color was a science, and a science that he had mastered. When Paepcke offered to supply anyone in Aspen with free paint for his house, only one resident accepted the offer because everyone assumed that Bayer would choose the colors.

The first buildings that Bayer designed for Paepcke were simple, linear, modestly proportioned. They were compatible with the Victorian townscape to the point of being nearly invisible. They were meant to serve as examples for other architects, but virtually no one else could or would follow his lead. In order to keep his stage harmonious, Bayer advocated strict planning and zoning ordinances in the city and county, and an architectural review committee that could reject any design it found unharmonious.

Unlike most artists, Bayer is first an intellectual. His studios have always been as immaculate as operating theaters. His lithographs look like color charts—very advanced, but charts nonetheless. His sculptures seem less inspired than they seem aesthetic principles carefully worked out and applied. His works are wonderful to see in the way that the resolution of a debate is wonderful to see, but there is no visible passion in it. I have seen passion in the man, seen his eyes flash, his hands chopping the air in two, but I have not seen it in his work.

Bayer was at odds with Aspen from time to time, but he seemed in absolute conjunction with Paepcke. When they stood together, hands in pockets, heads tilted congenially, talking quietly, nodding frequently, one sensed that sort of profound understanding that is at the heart of all enduring friendships. They were imagining something together: a perfect place, and they were joined as much by their failures as by their successes.

In 1953 Aspen was the handiwork of "Walter P. Possible who made everything in Aspen Paepcke," in the words of one local wit. Paepcke brought skiing and culture to Aspen and, as surely, brought me and others like me. But we simultaneously revered and resented him. That is the fate of Big Daddies. They are indispensible and they are therefore part blessing, part menace. Naturally, Walter Paepcke kept a regal distance between himself and the rest of us; and naturally, when he suggested that he knew better than we did, we agreed; and naturally, the relationship was a little strained.

There was a terrible lassitude in the people of Aspen when Paepcke arrived, and there was another kind of lassitude in those of us who followed him to Aspen. The natives could not seem to get going. The newcomers could not seem to settle down. In the midst of such people, it is easier to rule than to govern. We weren't ready for democracy, and Paepcke cared nothing for the democratic process, and so we were made for each other.

3∧
A Gathering of Fugitives

N EARLY EVERYONE I met in Aspen that summer was
a fugitive. The natives by merely staying put had
escaped not only the promises, but the demands of postwar American life. The newcomers were, for the most
part, either fleeing conventional jobs, responsibilities
and slots, or rejecting America and chasing after that
boundless frontier where they could, they believed, literally reinvent themselves, start at the beginning again
and make something quite different from what had been
in store for them back home.

In the summer of 1953, I worked for Berko-Henry
Studio. Ferenc Berko and Patrick Henry had nothing in
common but their disdain for the conventional way of
things. The possessor of a legendary name, Henry had
married a young Omaha heiress, moved from Omaha to
Aspen, and lost her to another man. Tall, handsome,
melancholy, he was the sort of man who could break
your heart, but was more apt to break his own and blame
you. Berko had been born in Hungary, educated in London and seasoned in Paris and India before coming to
America to teach at the Art Institute in Chicago. He
didn't much like America. His handwriting was tight,
neat and microscopic, like that of a scholar.

Both men were photographers. For Henry it was a passing occupation; for Berko it was occupation, passion, livelihood, everything. They took pictures of mountains and wildflowers and anything else in Aspen that might make nice post cards. Berko also took photographs of nude ladies and white stones and toothless old men. He would come out of the darkroom, hold his negatives an inch from his nose, squint at them in the light, and go back into the darkroom. He fairly vibrated with impatience. He knew that he was good and wanted all the glory and ease that were due him.

Berko's notions of commerce were, at best, haphazard, and Henry was already losing speed. Five days a week, from 2:00 to 6:00 P.M., I sat behind a counter under the stairs in the Jerome lobby and sold post cards, photographs and toys imported from Europe by Berko's wife. The counter, the display, the assortment of post cards, photos and toys all had an improvised look, as if it were an eccentric's hobby, when in fact it was two families' livelihood.

FREDRIC "FRITZ" BENEDICT first saw Aspen when he was serving with the Army's 10th Mountain Division. After the war he came back, sold his car, and bought Red Mountain, a vast shaggy slope that rises out of the valley like a wall and faces Aspen Mountain. Originally from Wisconsin, Benedict studied with Frank Lloyd Wright at Taliesin, where he was called "Gentle Spirit," became Aspen's first architect, contractor and wheeler-dealer. With his brother-in-law Herbert Bayer, he did some buildings for Paepcke. On his own, he did whatever he could find to do. He turned a barn on Red Mountain into a house and sold it, then bought the Bowman Block, a crumbling Victorian building, and restored the facade faithfully, while turning the inside into modern offices and apartments. For a time the Bayers owned half of the Bowman Block, and though the two men worked together successfully, Benedict had a much looser, more intuitive sense of things. His building crew consisted of ski instructors, bartenders and waiters. His building sites were like parties—cheerful, haphazard, everyone learning as he went along. Bayer liked glass, metal and brick. Benedict showed an early preference for native materials—stone, wood, timbers. The buildings he did with Bayer were spare. His own buildings were extravagant, eclectic, each made to suit the site and the moment. He would try anything.

Benedict's wife, Fabienne, and her half-sister, Joella Bayer, seemed equally as adventurous. The daughters of Mina Loy, an English poet whom Ezra Pound declared was all brains and no heart, they grew up among the avant-garde in Paris. Mrs. Benedict and Mrs. Bayer were as different as their husbands. Mrs. Benedict has an anarchic disposition, a taste for lost causes and complex pranks. She worked for British Intelligence during the war, married, and came to America. Her sister, in whom queenly pretensions and generous impulses combined, married Julien Levy, a tireless champion of the avant-garde. The couple moved to New York, where the Julien Levy Gallery became the American outpost for the modernist movement that emerged out of Mina Loy's circle. But by the time the sisters arrived in Aspen with their second husbands, they had the sort of practical intelligence, stamina and ironic wisdom that attaches to survivors. They did whatever they had to do, whether it was office bookkeeping or dining with a boring eminence at the Paepckes'. They had grown up on the run, and had stopped in Aspen. Here, they said, we will have our way.

This will be the last stop. They had determination in common, and ambition, but they had differences, too. Mrs. Benedict has a French temperament—volatile, unpredictable, outrageous, while Mrs. Bayer's nature is more Germanic—earnest, reliable, solemn. They constantly surprise each other.

Among such people, I was never sure that summer whether Aspen was the very edge of the world or its heart, the last outpost or the first rebel encampment.

THE PAEPCKES, the Bayers and the Benedicts, the Berkos and the Henrys all wanted to succeed in their fashion, but there were many people in Aspen whose fear of success was impressive. The efforts of Joan and Shady Lane to avoid success were already legendary. Mrs. Lane was a veteran of both the Women's Army Corps and the Junior League. Her husband and a fellow–10th Mountain Division veteran, one-time Olympic racer Steve Knowlton, founded the town's first ski shop. The moment the store began to succeed, Lane sold his interest, bought several acres of land on the Roaring Fork, and began building a house room by room. The Lanes bought their clothes at the thrift shop, scavenged lumber, and found furniture at the dump. They often rode the mountain in their old jeep, gathering up mine timbers, bricks and almost anything else they saw, and they were celebrated. Mr. and Mrs. Thoreau, making a house, wardrobes, a library and a life out of second-hand goods.

ALMOST EVERY newcomer to Aspen was doing something that he had never done before. Most of the menials —the waiters and bus boys and store clerks and bellboys —were at least as intelligent, well born and well-educated as their employers, and most of them were

more spirited than disciplined. Though they needed the
money, they didn't need the jobs. If they liked their
employers and their customers, they would spare nothing, but if they didn't like him or her or them, they
would do nothing. In those years Aspen was as un-
stratified as a place can be. The waiter who brought your
drinks one night in the Red Onion might be your dinner
partner the next night. In fact there were no menials.
There were simply young people pretending to be menials for a while. It was a game that some tourists and some
employers never understood.

But many of the employers were new to their voca-
tions too. A Vassar graduate ran Little Percent Taxi
Company. A former opera singer opened a restaurant. A
rich boy from St. Louis opened a bookstore. The former
wife of a Hollywood director, an Englishwoman of extraordinary energy, ran a boutique and a nursery school.
A former Longines executive became a baker. Still, lug-
gage got carried, beds got made, eggs got fried, fishing
rods got repaired, dishes got washed. Only people of
Germanic disposition, like Paepcke and Bayer, were
upset by these freewheeling ways.

Three afternoons a week, most of the menials and
employers along with the Paepckes went to the Aspen
Amphitheater, a giant white, orange and blue tent
erected over a concrete bowl. Set in a meadow on a bluff
overlooking the Roaring Fork, it had been designed by
Eero Saarinen, one of the era's leading architects, for
what may have been the decade's most preposterous
cultural event, the Goethe Bicentennial Convocation.

In 1948 Chicago's chancellor Hutchins and other
scholars organized the Goethe Bicentennial Foundation.
Its purpose was to stage some event that would simul-

taneously celebrate the 200th birthday of Johann Wolfgang Goethe, the German poet and philosopher; honor "the universal man, transcending the partial, provincial and passing" in a place where man's relationship to nature could be clearly seen; and restore unity to the Western world's intellectual community, which had been terribly divided by the war. Paepcke convinced Hutchins and the others that Aspen would be an ideal site for the convocation.

Never a man to stint, he then persuaded Goethe's most revered disciple, Albert Schweitzer, to come to Aspen from his clinic in the African jungle. It was Schweitzer's only visit to America. Spanish philosopher José Ortega y Gasset came to America for the first time too. England's delegation was led by poet Stephen Spender. Pulitzer Prize–winning playwright Thornton Wilder was at the head of a large group of Americans. Wilder also served as Schweitzer's translator. Fred Glidden told me later that when Wilder stood beside Schweitzer, a kind of magic occurred and the two men became one instrument whose only function was to honor a dead German genius. Sixteen concerts were performed by the Minneapolis Symphony under conductor Dimitri Mitropoulous, with such soloists as Arthur Rubinstein and Gregor Piatigorsky.

Only seventy years had passed from the moment that the first band of prospectors and their wives celebrated their first Christmas in Aspen in Henry Gillespie's tent to the moment that Schweitzer and Wilder stood in Saarinen's tent to celebrate "universal man." In those seventy years, the world had changed and moved, but Aspen had not moved any closer to it. It was still off there to one side, going its own way.

THE TENT became the concert hall for Paepcke's Aspen
Music Festival and School. Every summer the canvas
was raised, and three afternoons a week for ten weeks,
chamber music and symphonic works were performed.
Used to dark and earnest halls like the Syria Mosque in
Pittsburgh and Carnegie Hall in New York, I found the
tent, full of light and sweet summer air, bewitching.
Paepcke brought musicians of some reputation to Aspen
to perform and teach, offering music students opportunities to study and work with people they had only previously seen on the concert stage. It sometimes made for
curious alliances, as when fourteen-year-old student pianist James Levine found himself accompanying Met
baritone Mack Harrell in practice sessions.

In the summer, students and soloists practiced wherever they could—in houses, garages, empty rooms in the
opera house, in student dormitories in downtown Aspen,
in stands of trees along the river. Not all of it was good
music, of course, and a bad run on the violin was often
immediately followed by a run of sighing or swearing.
The music students were as different from Aspen's resident young people as the tortoise is from the hare. They
were pale, oddly dressed, tending to black shoes and
horn-rimmed glasses, and they were very serious. We
made fun of them sometimes and worse of them other
times. When a young violinist refused to go out with a
young Aspen resident, he and some friends wrote JEW
on the wall of her house in thick black paint.

JACK WARNER, MY FIRST true friend in Aspen, lived a
very different life from the Bayers and Benedicts. He
had no money, no things, no car, and his entire wardrobe
was contained in a duffel bag. He worked on the ski
patrol in the winter and in the stage show at the Golden
Horn restaurant in the summer. The show was very sim-

ple. Warner and several other men in Levi's and sneakers just stood on the small stage and moved their mouths in sync with records by such stars of the time as Frankie Laine and Jo Stafford.

He wasn't related to Hollywood's Jack Warner, nor, to hear him tell it, to anyone. I asked him once where he was from; he said he wasn't from anywhere. Like many young Aspen residents, his life began when he entered the valley. There was no past, no future. There was simply the moment, and he did what he could with it. He withheld everything except affection. He spent most of his day in the White Kitchen, a small plain cafe with a counter, eight stools, a profane proprietress and an endless supply of strong cheap coffee. Everyone talked to everyone else in the White Kitchen, but they didn't talk about anything that mattered, and they never asked questions. It was something like those scenes in western movies in which travelers stand at a bar for a while and drink, and then move on.

One afternoon a big black limousine cruised down Main Street. The Jerome bar regulars said it was President Eisenhower, but it turned out to be Ethel Merman. Warner, who had previously been offhand about his summer occupation, saying only that playing a fool was better than working as a waiter, was electrified by the news. He was convinced that she would come to the Horn, and spent the afternoon rehearsing the male half of one of Merman's more celebrated duets, "You're Not Sick, You're Just in Love." She did come to the Horn, Warner asked her to sing with him, and she did. Nearly all of Aspen was present, and when Merman and Warner finished, there was thunderous applause. Merman smiled, bowed, thanked Warner, and went back to her table. That was all there was. Warner claimed it was sufficient, but I knew that he had expected her to take him to New York to star with her in her next show. That was the way it happened in the movies, and we believed in the movies in the way we believed in Aspen.

Much of the valley was still in agriculture. Hereford cattle, sheep, hay and potatoes were the major crops. Cowboys who worked for cattle ranchers were superior to cowboys who worked for sheepmen. Some of the ranches had been bought by rich men from the East and Midwest. The leading old ranchers were the Vagneurs. Their forebears had arrived in the valley in the 1880s and homesteaded a huge sweep of land near Woody Creek, ten miles west of Aspen. There was a kind of tension between the lifetime ranchers and the new ranchers. The old-timers said that the rich men were simply playing at ranching. These soft city people, they said, threw money at a problem, while true cowmen got down in the dirt and grappled with it. At rodeos, it was noted, the rich men stayed on the fence with their friends. The truth was that ranching was a hardscrabble business at that altitude in that climate, and the old-timers barely made it from year to year. They simultaneously envied the rich men and thought they were fools.

The rodeo was the Old West's last stand in Aspen. The creaking of bridles and saddles, the slap of leather on leather, the clanging of metal, the sizzle of ropes whizzing through the air, the grunting of men and animals, the dust and heat, the snap of a bone in man or beast that was like a pistol shot were all at odds with the newly refined airs of the place. The cowboys lived as hard as they rode, saw Saturday night as another bronc to be ridden down, and got mean when they drank. Somehow, skiers and eggheads had got control of their turf, and they hated it.

IF THE FUGITIVES had a hero, it was Tom Weld. He moved through Aspen like a prince, was president of the Aspen Ski Club, seen from time to time with Toni Paepcke. In the summer he worked as a carpenter, wore cut-off overalls with tools hanging out of every pocket. In the winter he worked on the ski patrol, skiing in every kind of weather. Tall, graceful, wry, with the face of a star, he was too fine not to be occasionally arrogant, in the way that all the blessed are arrogant. But there was in him too a kind of hesitancy that signified an unreadiness or unwillingness to accept either the responsibilities or the privileges of his rank.

The Welds are an old American family, rich, aristocratic, proper Bostonians. Weld had gone to Harvard, then left it all behind and come to Aspen. He drove a beat-up red pickup truck, lived in a rented room, and was very happy. His family understood nothing. They urged him to get a proper job. He said he would give them a summer and hired on as a geologist at a mine in Nevada. I don't even know what they mined there. I only know that six weeks after he left Aspen, Tom Weld fell down a mine shaft and was killed instantly. Someone went and brought his truck back to Aspen. He was buried in the family plot in a Boston cemetery. All of Aspen mourned its lost prince, and blamed America for killing him.

ASPEN SEEMED at odds with its past now, but more at odds with America, reading its promises in an eccentric way, going in another direction, frankly elitist in its absorption with unmaterial rewards—uncluttered vistas, a pastoral pace, hikes beyond the wildflowers to high windy places, concerts in the tent, communion with geniuses like Adler. It was another kind of frontier, closer in spirit to Revolutionary America of 1776 than to postwar America. Here in the heart of the most material-istic nation in the history of humankind was a town so bent on responding in another way to the imperatives of the times that it built its economy on classical music, scholarly debates and snow.

4∧
Looking Down

I F THE JEROME POOL was the summer headquarters for most of Aspen, the Jerome bar was its winter headquarters. It remained much as Jerome B. Wheeler had made it. Tile floors, walls of dark wood and bordello wallpaper, the bar ornate, polished, a silvery mirror at its center. On winter afternoons it was hot and hectic. Its large windows on Main Street steamed up. People in ski clothes, their heavy boots unlaced, their faces red from the cold and exertion, crowded up to the bar or sat around tables drinking and telling extravagant stories about their exploits on the mountain. When Freidl Pfeifer and Fred Iselin appeared in the bar, they were received in the way film stars are received. They were the kings of the mountain.

Pfeifer came to America from Austria in the mid-thirties. He taught skiing at Sun Valley, served in the 10th Mountain Division, and came to Aspen in 1945. His alpine expertise combined congenially with Paepcke's business acumen, and together they organized the Aspen Skiing Corporation. Paepcke found investors in Aspen, Denver and New York, but the bulk of the capital came from his brother-in-law Paul Nitze, a New York investment banker. Pfeifer designed the mountain and organized the Aspen Ski School with his Sun Valley chum, Iselin. By the winter of 1946, with the opening of the world's longest chairlift on the immaculately designed Aspen Mountain, the Aspen Skiing Corporation was in business.

The first work on the mountain had been done ten years before when André Roch spent eight months in Aspen. Roch gave free ski lessons to children, organized the Aspen Ski Club with a group of local skiers, and designed the mountain's first trail. Frank Willoughby, a mining engineer and the son of a former Aspen mayor, organized townspeople and obtained the help of the Work Projects Administration. A trail was cut, and a boat tow was hauled up the slope by a half-inch cable, two mine hoists and a gas motor. The tow carried twenty people at a time and tickets cost 10 cents.

Roch Run dropped 2,700 feet in a mile and three-quarters. A ski magazine called it "one of the steepest runs in the world," and warned, "only experts can ride its slopes. . . ." In 1941 the National Ski Association Annual Alpine Championships were run on Aspen Mountain.

The ski instructor was adored by women, envied by men, only occasionally overtaken by that ennui that afflicts a mature man when he suddenly realizes that shouting "bend your knees" six hours a day at strangers is not a good way to live. Most of the instructors were young and strong. They didn't care much about money and could carouse all night and ski all day, but they only reigned four months of the year. When the lifts closed in April, they became carpenters, bartenders and real estate salesmen, went unheralded through spring, summer and fall. Only ski-meisters Pfeifer and Iselin could make a life of it.

They were like two aspects of the same phenomenon. Short, tightly made, with thick, slick black hair and a face as brown as old leather, Pfeifer was the brains of the mountain. Iselin, a handsome, ironic, middle-sized Swiss, was its heart. Together they made a ski school from a motley crew that ranged from a stone-jawed Austrian woodcutter to a Pasadena playboy.

In addition to co-directing the Ski School, Iselin opened Aspen's first travel agency, wrote an elaborate ski manual *Invitation to Skiing,* and helped his wife Elli, herself a ski instructor, run a chic ski shop. When anyone famous came to Aspen, Iselin had him or her sign a board in the shop and burned the autographs into the wood. There were many names there by the time I first saw it: Norma Shearer, Lana Turner, and Lex Barker, along with Mortimer Adler, Walter Reuther and Charles Percy. Celebrity and glory mattered to Iselin, but he was, most of all, a worker, rushing from this enterprise to that as if the devil were after him.

JAMES BOND was a hero to the rest of America then. Outside Aspen, people were whispering about the sexual revelations in the Kinsey Reports, *Sexual Behavior in the Human Male and Female.* Russia exploded its first hydrogen bomb. "How Much Is That Doggy in the Window?" "I Believe" and "Stranger in Paradise" were the most popular songs. Someone proved that the Piltdown man was a hoax. There were Cinemascope screens in movie theaters.

Skiing in the 1950s appealed primarily to people who were anxious for authentic thrills. As America boomed, Aspen residents and visitors skied, marked the beauty and serenity and singularity of the place in frequently rowdy ways, and mocked the mediocrity and conformity that had overtaken the nation. Most of the people who came to ski in Aspen in those years were as alien from the American mainstream as Aspen's residents were. Above all, they were self-ordained elitists. Whether poor poets or rich bankers, Aspen's winter visitors skied hard and possessed at least a vestigial romanticism and an admiration for grace under pressure. If they were rich, they skied, sailed, went on safari to Africa, led constantly invigorating lives, but were capable too of bad manners, arrogance, stupidity, bigotry and contempt for anyone they thought inferior to themselves. If they were poor, they were apt to be humorless, in awe of their own purity and genius, superior in the manner of monks. They were zealots who would occasionally walk up the mountain to prove their superiority to it. They ate everything on their plates because they had paid for it, and they were rotten tippers.

Knights and ladies, priests and nuns. Unsanctified, desperately odd, at ease only when they were uncomfortable, looking at life through heated eyes, they resembled those gaunt driven people who have sailed around the world alone or climbed a mountain in a blizzard.

They were at once like and unlike Aspen residents. One could see the differences and similarities every afternoon in the Jerome bar. The visitors generally had more money than the locals, but they were stingier with it. They dressed in tweeds and flannels like English gentry, while locals dressed in Levi's like students. Visitors were inclined to truckle to visiting and resident celebrities. I once watched a millionaire banker make a fool of himself over a fashion photographer, even as a local was making a fool of her. Visitors regarded European racers with awe, but locals said they dressed like fops and had the brains of canaries.

It was always an uneasy relationship: the visitors were used to being treated with a certain deference, and the locals were, for the most part, incapable of deference. Tourism was Aspen's primary source of money, but if locals had cared about money, they would not have been in Aspen. Still, because they had in common a love for skiing and a disdain for the ordinary American way of things, visitors and residents managed to abide together with reasonable good humor.

Paepcke's Aspen was made for this eccentric elite, the handful of people who fervently enjoyed sport and art. Determined to preserve the small scale and unique character of Aspen, he rejected anything that might cause it to grow too rapidly or carelessly as well as anything that might sully it. Its purity was, after all, its primary asset. On that basis he approved the 1950 Federation Internationale de Ski (FIS) championships, the most elite contest of the era, but rejected the 1952 winter Olympics. He turned down a request from Lowell Thomas, then the most famous news commentator in America, to do a series of broadcasts from the stage of the Wheeler Opera House because it would draw national attention to Aspen. But he liked a *New York Times* story that concluded, "The programs of the Aspen Institute bear witness to the nature of a project which may logically result in the establishment of one of the most important centers for arts and ideas that this country knows." Thomas talked to everyone; the *Times* addressed itself to the elite.

In postwar America, where there seemed to be no such thing as too much, Aspen's view of itself was at least heretical. Quality and quantity were perceived as opposites in perpetual conflict with each other. Implicit in nearly everything was the elevation of quality over quantity. If the quantity of skiers on Aspen Mountain increased beyond a certain limit, the quality of skiing was bound to decline. Likewise if too many people visited or moved to Aspen, the place would surely become less pleasant. Personal ambitions that were based on even the most benign exploitation of Aspen's assets were frowned on.

The Paepckes, Bayers, Benedicts, Gliddens, Pfeifers, Iselins and the rich ranchers all lived very well. The rest of us, by ordinary standards, did not. But they were ambitious, in a nice way, and we were not, in any way, so it seemed reasonable, and we accepted it without rancor or even thought. The fact that there were quite literally no opportunities for any of us to do what we had been trained to do, no jobs at all between low menial and high professional, no jobs for us that required skill or passion, was, in fact, a relief to us. We were all under Paepcke's wing and content to stay there. "One big happy family," someone said. We may be menials, we said, but we reside on Olympus.

THE ONLY young people who exhibited any ambition at all were racers. They were generally poor and hungry, or rich and spoiled, and they were never quite first-rate. By the fifties, Aspen was lodged securely in the top rank of American ski towns, and some of the world's top skiers lived there; but the town's young racers, like the rest of us, lacked some essential grit, and tended to be more temperamental than talented.

The town's top racer in the early 1950s was Max Marolt, a chunky, sullen native. He was good, but never good enough. Both his older brother and his younger brother were racers, and later became leading ski coaches; but Max wanted only to be the champion, and had neither the will or the skill to do it.

When Max didn't make the 1954 FIS ski team, towns-people raised money and sent him to Europe to compete as an independent. It was an unprecedented act, and the American ski hierarchy was outraged at its hubris. Aspen, they said, was part of America and should give whatever support it could muster to the American team. It would be wonderful to report that Max won every-thing, but he acquitted himself no better than the town had. Both lost face.

Ski bums outnumbered ski racers by twenty to one in Aspen. When they could, they worked as well as played on the mountain. Other times, they barreled around America on recapped tires. At a moment's notice, one or several ski bums would pile into a wreck of a car and drive nonstop across the country. They had no money and had to be as ingenious on the road as they were in Aspen. A carload of ski bums would wear down on the western race circuit and then flop exhausted on Carmel beaches or in Big Sur, or take over a couch in someone's San Francisco living room for a night or a month. Others went east, moving frantically through the night to the jazz beat on their car radios, paused, turned around, and came back. Like Jack Kerouac and his beat friends, they were on the road, but it was restlessness rather than a melancholy quest for truth that drove them.

We wore our voluntary poverty like a medal and boasted of our moral superiority. I once suggested to a young law student that he abandon the law and come to Aspen where, I said, he could work as a carpenter. He said that he didn't want to be a carpenter, he wanted to be a lawyer. I said that carpentry was a higher vocation than the law. He said I was crazy and went back to law school.

THE NATIVES OF ASPEN, most of whom had been born poor and therefore saw nothing romantic about it, thought we were crazy too. They resided somewhere between the menials and the leaders. They did the hard work of the town—plumbing, wiring, hauling coal, storekeeping. In their stores one found nuts and bolts instead of Venini glass and Irish sweaters. They were hard, suspicious people who saw the revival simultaneously as one last chance to make it and a rich man's trick. Some of them had already given up. More men than women had given up.

It was not uncommon to see a woman going off to work in the morning as her husband went off to spend the day at the Jerome or the Red Onion. These men were invariably red-faced, furtive and sad. Drinking did not improve them in any way, or even cheer them up. It just made them more furtive, and forced smarmy grins from them. Aspen's resurrection had come too late for them and was, in a way, a further affront. Paepcke had come to town and almost overnight done what they couldn't do in decades. Now they no longer had even the solace of talking about their plans for the place over their endless bourbons and branch water and boilermakers. It was a rude blow and pushed them further into their cups. Their wives had taken over their responsibilities, strangers had taken over their town. There was nothing left for them.

Their wives worked because they had to. Newly arrived women worked in surprising numbers too. Some because they had to, others because they wanted to. A pioneer community is inevitably made as much by women as by men, and Aspen was a kind of pioneer community. A number of city and county offices—the offices that required neat handwriting and mathematical skills—were held by women. There were also women ski instructors, lodge owners, photographers, architects and shopkeepers. One of the town's leading chefs was a woman who had once been a Foreign Service officer. One of its first real estate brokers was a woman. Ranchers' wives labored as long and hard as their husbands. Wives often helped their husbands remodel, refurbish or build houses.

Women played a decisive role in the creation of the strong sense of community that developed in the postwar years. They helped make a place in which everyone —young and old, rich and poor, native and newcomer— could feel at home. In those years there were virtually no social or economic divisions. Postwar Aspen was newly born, unprecedented, unstructured. No women's movement, no calculation put the women of Aspen in motion beside the men. They were present. They were vigorous and devoted. They were needed.

THE PROFESSIONAL people who began emigrating to Aspen were bound to be somewhat unusual, as life in Aspen offered neither much money nor many challenges. A Californian, Dr. Robert Barnard, became the town's second general practitioner and surgeon. He dressed like a rich rancher, had the vocabulary of a hipster, raced sports cars and collected antique cars, bought land, built houses, lived in them for a while and sold them, and turned up at nearly every public forum with a very strong opinion on the subject at hand. He was engaged in as many levels of life as he could find in Aspen, and numbered among his friends ski patrolmen, rich ranchers, old women, cowboys, divorcées and chefs. They all called him "Bugsy." Stocky, thick-featured, noisy, he had the build of a boxer, and Aspen was his mistress, sparring partner, and, from time to time, his opponent.

Declaring that the people of Aspen needed a voice on the board of directors of the Aspen Skiing Corporation, he talked himself onto the board and battled for better pay for patrolmen and reasonable lift ticket prices for residents.

Barnard's first wife was a doctor. His second was a divorcée whom he met during a two-year tour with the Navy in Panama. But Aspen was his primary passion. It came before marriage, before medicine, before everything.

ASPEN HAS ALWAYS been an ideal arena for the people sociologist Philip Slater was talking about when he said, "The American imagines himself to be alone on the continent." It attracts people whose behavior is as extreme as the weather.

A middle-aged man decided to blow up an anthill in his yard. The blast shattered every window in the neighborhood and gave him a terrific thrill, but killed only a few ants.

Offended by a ski merchant, a man backed his station wagon up to the merchant's store, took every pair of skis in the place, and went home. Only a telephone call from the sheriff warning that he could be charged with grand theft and sent to jail persuaded him to return the skis. The incident had no visible effect on the merchant.

A rather melancholy Irishman who thought that the sheriff was interfering in his personal problems shot the sheriff's car, breaking the lawman's heart.

A one-legged old man sold coal, green meat, gray candy and the Sunday *New York Herald-Tribune*. I asked him why he sold the *Trib*, meaning that it didn't seem of a piece with his other goods. He said, "I never liked the *New York Times.*"

A young woman of dignified mien was seen from time to time sliding down the bannister of the Jerome stairway "because it was there."

A waitress in the Jerome grill entertained herself on slow mornings by hanging pieces of fresh meat in the mouths of the deer and elk heads on the wall.

Someone invented a version of baseball that required the players to drink their way around the bases.

Freddie "Schnickelfritz" Fisher got rich and famous leading a band that employed washboards, saws, car horns and other anti-musical devices in movies, in nightclubs and on the radio. One day he left it all behind, and set out with his wife and children in a car and trailer to begin again. Freddie "The Fixer" Fisher became Aspen's Renaissance man of repairs. He got most of his supplies and equipment at the dump, and invented a way of electroplating aspen leaves to make jewelry that was sold in stores under signs that read, "Made by Freddie Fisher and God." He bred chickens for a while in his garage. When asked why he'd given up fame and fortune, he said, "I got tired of the God damn good life."

IN THE EARLY FIFTIES no one in Aspen was getting rich or famous. No great work of art, no great idea emerged from those blessed precincts, but tourists in adequate numbers in both winter and summer supported the pastoral pretensions of the residents, and the off-seasons were long and luxurious. The countryside and town were spacious, serene and unspoiled. It seemed the best of all possible worlds.

We talked of America in the way that families sometimes talk of the middle-aged uncle who has run off with a young woman of dubious habits. At parties, five or six of us could solve all of the American dilemmas before dessert. The bombs must be buried, the politicians locked up, the businessmen ignored or at least laughed at, the country clubs closed and the poets annointed. Then America would become the land of the free and the home of the brave, would become worthy of Aspen. We cherished our differences as if they were assets. We thought they were signs of our superiority. Hubris was in us as deep as Aspen was in the mountains. Americans were bigots who didn't like blacks or Jews or anyone not white, Protestant and prosperous. We were without prejudice. Americans saw Joe McCarthy as a hero. We saw him as a villain. Americans had a terrible appetite for things—cars and appliances and houses and clothes. We had exorcised our material lusts and achieved a fine purity. Americans were grimly scrambling for rooms at the top. We were content with the view from our high place.

We had only to look down to see the mess America was in. Physicist J. Robert Oppenheimer was dismissed from government service as a security risk, but the witch hunters were still riding high. Americans preferred thugs to geniuses. Hemingway won the Nobel Prize, but we knew that he had sold out years before. Only 6 percent of the world's population inhabited the United States, but those people owned 60 percent of the cars, 58 percent of the telephones and 45 percent of the radios in the world. Twenty-nine million families had television sets. The Supreme Court ruled segregation unconstitutional, but segregation continued. Americans, we concluded, loved things, hated each other, and hated genius most of all. A century before, Henry David Thoreau had urged people to "simplify, simplify," so that they did not

become "the tools of their tools." He was ignored of
course. The wise are always ignored in America, we decided.

There is a cycle that has repeated and repeated in
America. Word spreads—it is not always clear how—that
there is a remote, naturally congenial town where one
can live pleasantly and cheaply. Artists and writers move
to the place, achieve a rough harmony with the natives,
and go on with their work. Word spreads faster. The
place is described as beautiful, interesting, even exciting.
It takes on bohemian airs. Solemn intellectuals, liberated
clergymen, scholarly lawyers, earnest failures follow the
artists and writers. Rich people move in, buy old houses
and refurbish them, or build expensive new houses. As
the rich follow the bohemians and the mock-bohemians,
the middle class follows the rich. The place grows,
achieves a certain panache, and the little town becomes
a circus. In Aspen in the forties and fifties, despite all the
evidence to the contrary of once serene towns in New
England, Florida, the Southwest and California, we believed that the cycle would be short-circuited.

From its founding in 1879, there had always been in
Aspen a conviction that things were possible at those
exotic heights that were not possible at lower elevations.
We were a special and consecrated breed, and we would
have our way. Of course, we had a protector too. We
were playful and unreliable, and we cherished those
qualities in ourselves. But Walter Paepcke was wise and
reliable, and he was present, and he would keep the
American mob out.

5∧
Innocents at Work

ROBERT W. CRAIG'S nose, like Cyrano's nose, is his destiny. Craig is a tall lanky man, the big man whom everyone notices at a party or meeting. Without his fine nose, he might have succumbed to some ordinary way of life. He was attractive, intelligent, well-educated, capable of conventional success in sports, business, academe, and with women. *Life* magazine once named him one of America's most promising young leaders. But Craig never took the obvious way, never did those things that might have assured him of conventional success in his work or life, and his occasional failures have been more distinguished than most men's successes. He sometimes signs letters to friends, "Cyrano."

In the spring of 1954, when all that was left of winter was a patchy dirty crust of snow on the north side of houses and trees, Craig came back to Aspen. He'd gone off a year before with a group of mountain climbers to conquer K2, the world's second largest mountain. He returned with frozen toes and awful memories. A comrade had died and no one made it to the top. Now he looked around. He had a master's degree in philosophy from Columbia, had been an officer in the Navy and an instructor at the Army's Cold Weather Defense Command at Camp Hale. There was nothing to be made of any of that in Aspen. He had no job and no prospects, had been beaten nearly insensible by the mountain, but he had true improvisational skills and $40.

He set out to resurrect the *Aspen Flyer,* a mimeographed broadside that had been published six days a week until its previous publishers got bored. Craig bought the logo and mimeograph machine, and hired me. Before the first issue came out, he told me that he would be working for Walter Paepcke by the fall. I told him that if we did our job right, Paepcke wouldn't even be speaking to him by the fall.

Craig sold the ads, wrote some of the straight matter, ran the mimeograph machine, and distributed the *Flyer* around Aspen every morning. I wrote the rest of the straight matter and most of the ads, and cut the stencils. It was a long, long way from the *Pittsburgh Sun-Telegraph,* the Hearst newspaper where I began my career, but it was journalism of a kind and I was happy to be back.

The *Flyer* operated out of the kitchen in Waddy Catchings's house in downtown Aspen. Catchings had a Harvard degree and plenty of money and rented rooms to eligible bachelors. The other boarders that summer were a dapper Chicago man who had vowed never to work, and one of Joella Bayer's sons by Julien Levy who was working for the summer as an apprentice printer at the *Aspen Times.* My typewriter was permanently located on Catchings's kitchen table. The mimeograph machine was on his back porch. Our stencils, paper, ink, cigarettes and beer cans were everywhere. Catchings is a scrupulously organized man, so our daily commotion was hard for him to bear. Several times during the summer he came close to evicting us.

The *Aspen Times,* our competition, had been founded in 1881, was a daily until the late 1920s, and was owned in 1954 by Verlin Ringle, a well-meaning and cheerful man who admitted that he was a printer, not a journalist. The *Times* ran several pages of social notes, canned sermons and news stories that read like press releases. Editorials were rare and generally took the form of compliments to some civic group or other. Ringle held that the paper had no need of reporters, and it was true. The *Times* did not cover meetings, events or anything else. It was passive, respectful, peripheral, provincial.

It seemed important that the first issue of the *Flyer* give Aspen a sample of provocative journalism, and a likely target was on hand. Every June the town was the site of a convention of designers from all parts of the country, the International Design Conference in Aspen. It was another of Paepcke's inventions, but it seemed more solemn than serious. The conference always began on an Olympian level. By the end of the week, people said, some Big Question or other would be laid to rest. But inevitably, after a week of talks, lectures, movies, slide shows and seminars, the conferees would conclude that bad design in America was the fault of the people and go home happy, absolved again from blame. I wrote an acerbic essay, "Well-Designed Designers?" that suggested these priests of good taste were themselves badly designed and therefore incompetent.

Craig mimeographed and distributed the *Flyer* without reading it. He was astonished to receive a call at 8:00 A.M. from Joella Bayer scolding him for attacking well-heeled, influential visitors to Aspen. She suggested that the *Flyer* take a more positive line or cease publication. Craig assured Mrs. Bayer that it was a "lapse" and apologized. He was convinced that his life in Aspen was over, that Paepcke would, instead of hiring him, run him out of town, and that no one would even protest his explusion.

The *Flyer* immediately became a kind of house organ for Paepcke's enterprises: the music was the best in the world, the Institute speakers were uniformly brilliant, its seminars were the headiest stuff. By mid-summer, Craig had more invitations than he could handle.

THAT SUMMER, the word was out that the Festival was about to fly apart. Over dominoes with two members of the New Music Quartet, a chamber music ensemble, I heard it told that Paepcke was a dictator, a man who knew nothing about music or musicians. Both his conductor and his manager were toadies, claimed these highly excitable, temperamental young New Yorkers. They were plainly impatient with any sort of authority. I wanted to break the story in the *Flyer.* Craig said domino players were fundamentally unreliable.

On the eve of the annual summer rodeo, Paepcke decreed that rodeo events could not be scheduled on concert afternoons. The cowboys ignored the dictum and proceeded. Many townspeople cheered. Paepcke raged. The *Rocky Mountain News* headlined the dust-up MUSIC VS. MANURE. But it was deadly serious to Paepcke, most townspeople and the musicians. Paepcke called a series of urgent, heated, closed meetings in the opera house. The shouting could be heard from the street. When the meetings were over, there were as many versions of them as there had been people present. Paepcke announced that a new nonprofit corporation, the Music Associates of Aspen, had been formed to run the Festival and School. It would share some facilities with the Institute, such as the tent and the opera house, but would be financially and aesthetically independent.

No one was objective about the circumstances of the split. Some people, like the domino players, said the musicians forced it. Others said that Paepcke himself had deliberately triggered it so he could focus exclusively on the Institute. Others said it was a simple matter of money. Paepcke couldn't support and sustain both the Festival and the other Institute programs, so he chose to abandon the Festival while making it seem that he had been forced out by barbaric cowboys and arrogant musicians.

Paepcke had run a one-man show. His imperatives and sensibility had been primary, and the principal financial burden had been his too. At concerts the Paepcke family sat front and center in cushioned captain's chairs while everyone else endured hard benches. Under the direction of Courtlandt F. Barnes, Jr., the chairman of the board of the Music Associates, and his board members, democracy came to the tent. Barnes was a stockbroker whose real passion was music. He revered it and the people who made it sufficiently to give them power to set programs, hire and fire performers, and run the school while Barnes and his board handled the business side. Barnes, witty, light-hearted, something of a dandy, was an effective and shrewd peacemaker, and he immediately set up several committees of residents to assist the board in such areas as publicity, fund-raising and housing for the musicians.

A week after the summer season ended, Craig was named executive director of the Aspen Institute. I congratulated him, and I took the logo and mimeograph machine home with me, intending to go it alone, exposing all the rascals and bullies one by one. Catchings said he didn't care what I did as long as I didn't do it in his kitchen.

AFTER THINKING, experimenting, bringing a variety of people from a variety of fields to Aspen and talking to people ranging from Henry Luce of Time, Inc., to Ortega y Gasset, Paepcke had founded the Aspen Institute for Humanistic Studies as a kind of umbrella for all of his scholarly and aesthetic endeavors. He wrote: "Education, according to [Alfred North] Whitehead, should hold before us and sustain 'a vision of greatness,' the greatness of the human spirit and the works of man. To this educational objective, the Aspen Institute for Humanistic Studies is dedicated. The essence of its humanistic ideal is the affirmation of man's dignity, not simply as a political credo, but through the contemplation of the noblest works of man—in the creation of beauty and the attainment of truth.

"At the midpoint of the twentieth century, when men's lives are dominated more than ever by science, they need the elevation and liberation of a sound humanism. In a world which almost worships science and technology, we must rediscover the moral and spiritual truths which will enable man to control science and its machinery."

Albert Schweitzer was named an honorary trustee, and the board included Robert M. Hutchins, Ortega y Gasset, Thornton Wilder and scholars and businessmen. The summer of 1950 was a trial period for the Institute. Paepcke scheduled two months of lectures, seminars, forums and concerts. Among those present were Mortimer Adler, theologian Reinhold Neibuhr, psychiatrist Karl Menninger, writers Clifton Fadiman and Jacques

Barzun, painter Josef Albers, photographers Ansel Adams, Eliot Porter and Dorothea Lange, architect Louis Kahn, designer Charles Eames and labor leader William Gomberg. This sort of mix was central to Paepcke's belief in what he called "cross-fertilization."

Ortega suggested that Paepcke aim for nothing less than "a total synthesis of human life," while Luce urged him to focus on what he called "the great unwashed American businessman" because ". . . men so exposed to basic issues, social, economic and religious, might not merely remain business leaders, but become leading citizens." Paepcke agreed with Luce and organized a program of executive seminars to bring businessmen together for two weeks of reading both classic and contemporary works and discussion with scholars, writers and politicians. Paepcke imagined he could create legions of enlightened businessmen like himself who would go forth from Aspen and perfect America. Achieving "a total synthesis of life" might have been easier.

Craig invited me to a cocktail party to welcome the next group of businessmen-students. Several dozen unstylish and earnest men and women, the usual handful of imported savants and some other townspeople were present. A bald man in pinstripes and glasses stuck out his hand and said, "Merriam, Omaha Gas." I shook hands with him and said, "Clifford, *Aspen Flyer.*" He thought I was serious. I abandoned him and approached the session's token labor leader. We talked for a while, I trying to get him to condemn the bosses who were playing intellectuals in the mountains for two weeks, and he trying to persuade me to go upstairs and bed down with him. We both failed, and I went home and wrote that the Institute notion, however idealistic, was doomed.

Paepcke was as different from the silver kings who built Aspen as he was from other big businessmen in postwar America, but though he thought small for Aspen, he thought very big for his Aspen enterprises. Some newcomers felt that his intellectual courtship of big businessmen in an anti-business town was at best a contradiction, at worst hypocritical, and in any event, futile. Some long-time residents found Paepcke autocratic, devoted to his own grand vision, but uninterested in their more ordinary dreams of money in the bank, a new car, college for their children. Paepcke had made a fortune before he got to Aspen, they said, but they were still waiting to make their fortunes. And if he had his way, they never would.

People speculated endlessly about his motives. Some said he was a kind of cultural megalomaniac who could not make music or paintings or poetry or new ideas and wanted to manipulate those who did. Others saw the Institute as a very elaborate device designed to ensure an unending supply of interesting dinner guests. The more cynical said that he was a very small fish in a very big pond in Chicago, but in Aspen he was the biggest fish of all. He was described simultaneously as arrogant and shy, a man of genius and a clever head hunter, a man passionately devoted to the life of the mind and a man trying merely to please his wife.

In fact, Paepcke was, in a town of innocents, the ultimate innocent. He believed that he could keep Aspen pure and could make American businessmen pure again. Most of us simply refused to grow up, but he wanted to remake America, to turn it away from things and back to ideas. He saw that America had got sidetracked too

early, had got down to business too soon, and he wanted
to raise it up as he had raised Aspen up. Paepcke's plan
worked better in theory than in fact. Year after year,
more and more businessmen came to be cleansed in the
mountains, but when they went back to America, it was
business as usual.

THE MEANNESS of life at lower latitudes was brought
home viciously when Jack Warner died suddenly in a
Denver hospital. He was young and strong, but he woke
up one day with a headache that bent him double with
pain and wouldn't go away. An Aspen doctor sent him
to Denver for tests. The tests were inconclusive. It might
be meningitis, or it might be a brain tumor, doctors said.
And so he died, proving again that beyond the mountains there were dragons.

The list of Aspen casualties was long in those years.
Tom Weld fell down a mineshaft. Warner died in a Denver hospital. Other favorite sons died of drink or in car
wrecks or avalanches, and the number of walking
wounded was considerable. I knew a young architect for
several years and never saw him sober. A man who spent
every winter in Aspen and skied like a champion was
drunk every day by breakfast. Even the local peeping
tom was a drunk. People regularly fell off mountains,
froze to death inches from safety, were smothered in
avalanches they had triggered, drove off cliffs, drowned
in whitewater, passed out in snowbanks, had every kind
of fatal accident.

It was not just that we were careless—though we
were, of course. It was that we were arrogant. We expected everything from the world and were unwilling to
offer anything in return. We insisted on having our own

way, and when one of us fell off a mountain, we blamed the mountain. If the road turned and one of us didn't, we accused the road of treachery. Generally and specifically we were innocent and the world was guilty.

The odd thing is that the world believed us, took us at our word, and liked us for it. America lost its innocence when it was still a child, when the Industrial Revolution overtook the American Revolution. It has been looking for it ever since. The Declaration of Independence stated the ideal: "We hold these truths to be self-evident; that all men are created equal; that they are endowed by their Creator with certain unalienable rights; that among these are life, liberty, and the pursuit of happiness." In a letter to his wife, John Adams put it more concretely: "I must study politics and war, that my sons may have liberty to study mathematics and philosophy, geography, natural history and naval architecture, navigation, commerce and agriculture in order to give their children a right to study painting, poetry, music, architecture, statuary, tapestry and porcelain."

But tempted by the tangible rewards of industrialism, America had gone straight from "politics and war" to "commerce" and stayed there. It had left its founders' dreams unfulfilled, abandoned the pursuit of happiness for the pursuit of money, violated itself in the most fundamental way, and it felt guilty. When America was prospering in the late nineteenth century, the 1920s, and the 1940s, it searched its soul, wondered where it had gone wrong. When it was poor in the years of the Great Depression, it struggled with its bad conscience. Always it looked for its lost youth, its lost innocence, its vanished purity.

Aspen, hung back in time, was still young, still innocent, still lovely, lithe and chaste, unmarked by history and all the pulls and tugs of ordinary American life, still inviolate.

There is only one monument to a national event in Aspen. It is a statue of a Civil War veteran. Aspen did not even exist during the Civil War.

6⌃
Power to the Players

I N 1955 the town moved to codify its innocence. The instrument was a zoning ordinance that said in effect that what was at that moment would be the measure for everything that might come along later. In the West End, for example, where existing yards were large, future yards must be equally large. New tourist accomodations could be built only in those areas of the city already devoted to such accomodations. Businesses would not be permitted outside the four square blocks of the business district. In that way the status quo would be preserved. Aspen would remain small, spacious and serene.

The ordinance was desired by Walter Paepcke, developed by Herbert Bayer, Fritz Benedict and Fred Glidden, and approved by the Aspen city council. It was one of the few instances in the 1950s of elected officials actually participating in the shaping of the place. Politics was a nearly superfluous activity in Aspen. The people who held office were more caretakers than powerbrokers or lawmakers. They saw to it that roads were repaired and plowed, taxes collected and disbursed in an orderly way, and other simple services performed with some efficiency. The same people held office for years without challenges from newcomers. This is not to say that these public servants did not guard their turf jealously, but that their ambitions for themselves and the place were limited. Truly important decisions were made in other arenas. Only when such decisions needed formal weight, needed legal standing, were the elected officials dealt in, and even in those rare instances their consent, not their advice, was requested.

Walter Paepcke never sought or held public office in Aspen. He didn't have to because he held all the high cards, and the way he played those cards had more impact, in both the short and long term, than anything the elected officials might do. He could and did orchestrate virtually everything of community significance by his management of the Aspen Skiing Corporation and the Aspen Institute. They were his creations and the primary instruments in the town's economic and social revival. When the 1952 Olympics committee wanted to stage the winter games in Aspen, they approached Paepcke, not the city fathers. When Paepcke needed official sanction for his plans, as with the 1955 zoning ordinance, he recognized the elected officials, but most of the time, he ignored them and went about the business of remaking Aspen independent of them.

The city fathers were small-town men, inarticulate, unsophisticated, and they were usually content to let Paepcke have his way. For pride's sake they might argue for a moment, but they never really crossed him and never refused to let him have his way, whether he wanted a pothole filled or a zoning ordinance passed. They were there because the city charter required a city council, regular elections and all the other stuff the democratic process in American small towns is made of. But in Aspen they weren't really needed. The men who patched the roads and drove the snowplows knew what they were doing and would go on doing it whether or not anyone sat at the council table. Tax matters were taken care of by two shy, giggly, but efficient women. The true direction of Aspen was set in the Jerome, or wherever Walter Paepcke happened to be. Bayer, Benedict and Glidden were his friends, his allies and his principal representatives in the community. They understood his vision of Aspen, admired it, and did everything they could to see that it was faithfully executed. In the mid-fifties, Glidden won a seat on the city council, thus bringing the vision inside city hall on a formal basis for the first time. A master of fiction, he made himself as slow and hesitant as his colleagues, managing thereby not to frighten them, but he had no more real clout as an elected official than he had previously had as one of Paepcke's compatriots.

It looked like a perfect scenario for trouble: one man with great power, a group of weak elected officials, a lazy electorate. But the man was wise, the officials were willing, and the electorate was very happy.

Things were somewhat livelier in the Pitkin County Courthouse. Two conservative Democrats ran the county. Tom Sardy, a man of modest temper, the local undertaker and co-owner with the Paepckes of Aspen Lumber and Supply was another staunch Paepcke ally. Orest Gerbaz, the sheep-ranching scion of a pioneer family, was a classic western figure—sardonic, shrewd, a formidable enemy and a valuable friend. Gerbaz didn't care much about culture or skiing, but he cared a great deal about money. He sold off his ranch in pieces and watched, with no apparent unhappiness, a gravel pit and a trailer court grow simultaneously near his house.

The third county commission seat was held by a succession of Republicans, but they never disagreed with

Sardy and Gerbaz, who believed in keeping taxes low, roads smooth and plenty of money in the bank. Sardy once said that he and his colleagues were just "housekeepers," and that was as it should be. Perhaps the county did not pass its own zoning ordinance in 1955 to complement the city's because such high-flown matters were not the province of housekeepers. Or perhaps it was because such an ordinance would have forbidden gravel pits, trailer courts and other profitable possibilities.

THE TOWN looked liberal in those days. In fact, a man whispered to me at a cocktail party that one out of every two people in Aspen was a Communist. When I asked him what so many Communists were doing in a ski resort, he shrugged and went off to whisper to someone else. But conservative natives had the edge in the voting booth. In elections, they prevailed. Adlai Stevenson, an old friend of the Paepckes, was trounced by Eisenhower in Pitkin County in 1952.

Disturbed by such apathy, Barbara Poindexter, a middle-aged widow of independent means, set about to raise the political consciousness of the town. On a bright summer afternoon, she brought together a crowd of residents she perceived as liberal to have drinks with Walter Reuther, perhaps the era's most dynamic labor spokesman. Reuther was to accompany Bob Craig, and Craig was chronically tardy. By the time they arrived, bedlam had overtaken Mrs. Poindexter's living room. A businessman was weeping in the corner about his wife's cruelties, a Festival musician was shouting about high-country philistines who came late to concerts, a blonde woman was talking to a curtain. Reuther saw immediately, if Mrs. Poindexter did not, that the opportunities for serious political discussion were limited, and he concentrated on the setting sun until he could escape gracefully. The liberal revolution went unrealized.

THE NATIVES, those people who had been born in Aspen and hung on through all the barren years, dreamed of an unencumbered frontier, of finally being able to strike it rich as their forebears had during the silver boom. The newcomers, those people who had followed Paepcke to Aspen, dreamed of a kind of utopia on the Roaring Fork where intelligent people could live well without capitulating to commerce, as most Americans had done. The natives' dream of a bonanza in the making was at odds with the newcomers' more refined vision, and the difference caused tiny fissures in the community. The newcomers objected to such things as gravel pits and trailer courts. The natives saw them as signs of progress. The newcomers agreed with Paepcke that the 1952 winter Olympics would bring too many people to Aspen. The natives disagreed; they wanted more people to come to Aspen. But the argument was not waged on the political level.

No one in Aspen in the 1950s, neither natives nor newcomers, saw politics as a crucial or even ideological endeavor. The people who held office were thought of not as politicians or leaders, but as managers, functionaries, clerks. The natives had been estranged too long from the hectic national political arena. The newcomers viewed politics with cynicism. The men who held office in the city and county were not themselves moved by the usual political drives. Of all of them, Gerbaz was the only one to openly seek and use power, but he used what power he had very selectively, and in a negative rather than a positive way. He wasn't *for* much of anything, but he was *against* anyone telling him or his friends what they could or couldn't do with their land, and he was *against* anyone, including the Federal government, trying to divert water out of the Roaring Fork Valley— unless, of course, the valley got something in return. In this sense, he was more pragmatist than politician.

The natives and the newcomers argued occasionally, debating these questions. But the arguments were personal and philosophical, not political. In the end, the questions were resolved by Paepcke anyway. As long as utopia was profitable, the natives and newcomers abided easily together despite their differences, though each thought the other somewhat backward.

WILLIAM R. DUNAWAY got off to a terrible start in Aspen. On a Friday in March 1956, he was fired as editor of *Skiing* magazine, headquartered in Denver. On Saturday, while competing in the Veterans' Downhill in Aspen, he flew off the course shouting, "There she goes!" seconds before he slammed into a mogul and shattered his left leg. Before he got out of the hospital, his wife asked for a divorce. But being a man of extraordinary hubris, he immediately set about to buy the *Aspen Times.* He had no money of his own, only the promise of some from his ex-mother-in-law. His leg was encased in plaster. Ringle had regularly rejected offers for the paper. But Dunaway prevailed.

Craig, an old friend of Dunaway's from their days at the University of Washington, suggested I meet the man. "His name is Bil with one l Dunaway," Craig said. Then he informed me that Dunaway wanted to consolidate our papers. Though I had no interest in a partnership, or in anyone who spelled Bill with one l, I met with him anyway.

Dunaway planned to print the *Flyer* on his presses, and to have me act as its editor and publisher with absolute control. I would also become managing editor of the *Times*. Trained as an economist, Dunaway had no newspaper experience. The only writing he'd done had been for ski publications. He was, however, cheerful and aggressive, and he saw things clearly while I did not.

After several intense meetings during which Dunaway talked, fidgeted, scratched and flung himself about as if his skin could not contain all of his ambitions, he informed me that if I did not join him, he would have to run me out of business. He had nothing against me personally, but if I chose not to work with him, then we would naturally be adversaries. It was an offer I couldn't refuse.

The *Times* building was one enormous room with desks in front, the linotype machine and old stone composing tables in the middle and the presses in back. The paper was printed on a flatbed press that had been hauled in pieces over the mountains in 1881. The job work—menus, posters, bills and the like that Dunaway said paid for our editorial adventures—was printed on small snapper presses. Along one wall was a bank of cases of lovely old wood-and-metal type. The windows on the east wall of the building looked directly into the Jerome garden.

The staff consisted of a printer who had previously smashed one hand in a snapper press, his wife, who ran the linotype when she was sober, and a ski bum who ran the big press on Thursdays. Titles meant nothing. Dunaway operated the folding machine and swept up when he was not selling ads. I sorted type, set headlines in a typestick, proofread and on Thursdays operated the hand-driven addressograph. Between us we also covered every beat in the county. Days were long and tempers short.

Accompanied by Dunaway, Ferenc Berko had recently taken several photos inside the water company storage tank. The photos showed debris, rat feces and other noxious stuff in the city's water supply. Dunaway appeared before the city council to announce that the photos would appear on the front page of the *Times*. The council naturally protested: the tourist season was just getting under way. Dunaway suggested that the city condemn the privately owned company and take it over. The council argued that free enterprise was sacred. Dunaway said the public's health was sacred too. He ran a picture. Soon afterward the city began a long effort to take over the water system, but the town's attitude toward the *Times* was set. Everyone had known the water was bad, but no one had said it out loud because it wasn't that bad. We were just "damn troublemakers."

One or the other of us turned up at every meeting, every sports event, every cultural event, every event of any significance with paper and pencil. We were frowned at before we even made a note. When our notes turned into news stories, and the news stories turned up in type in the *Times,* they were frequently and noisily denied. People denied statements and actions attributed to them. They accused us of bias, bad manners and plain stupidity. People cursed us on the street. A dignified middle-aged woman threw a cup of coffee halfway across a restaurant at me. Another woman slugged Dunaway at a cocktail party because she thought I had slandered her son. From time to time, our lives were threatened. From time to time, Dunaway said, "We can't have any friends," and there were times when we didn't have any friends.

Advertising boycotts became a favorite weapon. One restaurant owner who felt he'd been slandered in an editorial persuaded most of the town's restaurants to pull their ads. This boycott lasted for several months, but like all subsequent boycotts, it did not move Dunaway.

IN 1950 1.5 million people visited America's national forests; by 1960 6.6 million people were taking to the woods annually. In 1955 there were 200 symphony orchestras in America, an increase of 80 percent over fifteen years. Twenty-five hundred American towns had organized concert series and 35 million Americans attended at least one concert a year. The new affluence, the increase in leisure time, and America's escalating interest in the arts and sports all had an impact on Aspen. The Aspen Skiing Corporation, which had begun to capitalize on this new affluence, became Dunaway's favorite target.

Though he was its founder, Paepcke played a progressively smaller role in the Skiing Corporation. In the 1950s its president was William V. Hodges, an anxious and agreeable man; its vice-president was D. R. C. Brown, son of an Aspen pioneer; and its principal stockholder was Paul Nitze, Paepcke's brother-in-law. When the corporation's main lift broke down in 1957, effectively shutting down the mountain, Brown and Nitze refused to refund the cost of visitors' lift tickets. Residents finally organized a jeep lift and drove visitors up the back side of the mountain over an old mine road so they could ski down the front side. This incident, Dunaway said, vividly demonstrated the greed of the corporation. The residents were in the game for love, but the corporation seemed to be in it for the money. The enmity between the corporation and Dunaway enlarged.

BEYOND THE MOUNTAINS, life moved increasingly fast and seemed further and further removed from the life we lived in Aspen. We were unmoved by Fidel Castro's arrival on a Cuban beach: we knew nothing of the tropics. When Russia launched Sputnik, man was no longer earthbound. The earth itself had no bounds. Infinity was a fact that implied, on the one hand, a terrible randomness, a loosening of the cosmic bolts, and on the other, the promise of a frontier enlarged even beyond America's reach. The distance between Aspen and America seemed to be growing. Men were moon-bound, but we still sat around wood stoves on cold evenings.

There were rumblings of discontent in America, however—small signs that people out there saw what we saw. Such best sellers as *The Man in the Gray Flannel Suit, Peyton Place, Marjorie Morningstar* and *Some Came Running* implied that the nation was inhabited almost exclusively by conformists, hypocrites and money grubbers. The Gross National Product had escalated to nearly $400 billion by the middle of the 1950s. Efforts to desegregate schools in Little Rock drew soldiers into the Arkansas city to keep the peace. Joe McCarthy died. Something called rock 'n' roll was replacing the saccharine pop songs of the early fifties. Its rough driving beat seemed to grow out of a fundamental disaffection. Elvis Presley was no happier with America than the novelists were. But Elvis never caught on in Aspen.

Dixieland jazz—hot, mainstream, tailgate, traditional jazz—had captured the town. Although he had vowed never to perform again, Freddie Fisher formed a Dixieland trio with his son King on cornet and Walt Smith on piano. Fisher himself played clarinet and soprano saxophone. He also sang. They were the hottest act in town, moving with their followers from the Red Onion to the

Jerome and back. But one night, Fisher's songs got too ribald for the assistant manager of the Jerome, and the musicians were fired.

A jam session was set for the following night to honor Fisher, jazz and freedom of speech. The site—an enormous West End living room—was chosen, the essentials —a piano, piano tuner, ice and glasses—were marshaled, the neighbors were warned, and everyone in Aspen was invited.

Fisher kicked off at dusk with "Royal Garden Blues." A dark tapestry of a knight killing a dragon hung just over his head. The sunken bathtub was filled with ice. The room filled up. Smoke rose from 200, 2,000 cigarettes. Fisher and the other musicians grouped and regrouped and blew very hot. Every kind of booze had been brought to the party, and it was quickly consumed. Classical percussionist George Gaber hovered over his drums like an ecstatic Buddha, and Fisher himself smiled transcendently from time to time. People stood, sat, lay about. Drunk, very happy, I kissed a bearded man I had never seen before and never saw again.

At noon on the following day, the jazz king of Aspen was holding court in the post office and he said to me with a gleam in his eye, "You were having a very good time last night." I said, "Everyone was having a very good time last night." The jam session seemed to prove the efficacy of good times as a way of life.

Good times were profitable too. In 1958 Whipple Van Ness Jones, a man given to knickers and unblinking silences, carved the Aspen Highlands ski area out of the dazzling terrain in the Maroon Creek Valley southwest of Aspen. A Harvard graduate and one-time stockbroker, Jones put the Highlands together as carefully as he had once assembled stock portfolios. He brought Stein

Eriksen, an Olympic gold-medal winner and skiing's first golden boy, to Aspen to run the Highlands ski school and to perform. Every day at noon Eriksen flew off a jump, did a lazy graceful flip, and landed upright and smiling. It was clear he wasn't just another ski instructor. He was a star. Fritz Benedict designed the base building, an enormous triple A-frame that repeated the silhouette of the mountain. Jones installed Freddie Fisher in the nightclub.

The following year, Freidl Pfeifer, still restless, severed his connection with the Aspen Skiing Corporation and constructed a new ski area called Buttermilk on ranchlands he and his wife owned just west of Aspen on Highway 82. The new area drew skiers intimidated by the steep runs of Aspen Mountain and Aspen Highlands.

With the opening of the Highlands and Buttermilk, Aspen became the largest ski resort in America, and the lock that the Aspen Skiing Corporation had on the town was loosened. Obviously anyone with a mountain and money could play.

Jones was the first of a new breed in Aspen: the puritan playboy. There have always been playboys in America, the anti-puritan sons of puritan fathers. The puritan playboys were rich men who worked as hard as they played, as if to prove something to their fathers. They were enormously ambitious, but they hid their ambitions behind a kind of careless charm. They flew into Aspen in their own small sleek planes, skied for a weekend or a week, left, returned, became semi-residents, and sometimes residents.

Joseph B. Thomas IV was drawn to quixotic endeavors. Trained as an architect at Harvard, he dreamed of building inexpensive but beautiful tract houses. His first houses were inexpensive, under $20,000, but somewhat homely. He also flew small groups of people to mountaintops in a Cessna 180 equipped with skis. Kingsbury Pitcher, another of the breed, once said that Thomas "had been stuck on the top of every mountain within a forty-mile radius of Aspen."

Pitcher was the grandson of Otto Mears, a Russian immigrant who amassed a fortune from toll roads and railroads in southwestern Colorado during the mining era. He was a ski instructor, and owned a house in town and a ranch in Woody Creek. He never seemed to have any money, but he always had a plane, ten or twelve cars including some vintage Lincoln Continentals, and the ranch.

Pitcher and William Janss had grown up together in Pasadena. They had gone to Stanford and into the Air Force together, and they remained close friends. Billy Janss, who had been an Olympic skier, began to spend more and more time in Aspen and finally bought a house there. With his brother Edwin, he headed the Janss Investment Corporation, a Southern California land and cattle combine founded by their grandfather. The Corporation owned the vast Coachella Valley feed lot and developed such large Los Angeles subdivisions as Thousand Oaks.

Together these grandsons of pioneers set about to do some pioneering of their own in the Roaring Fork Valley. On surveying the crowd in the Sundeck, a restaurant on top of Aspen Mountain, one afternoon in 1957, the Janss brothers and Pitcher decided it was time to develop a major new Colorado ski area. Pitcher acted as point man and went looking for a likely mountain. He roamed Colorado's front range, but found nothing suitable. That summer he was, in his own words, "jouncing around on my hay baler in Woody Creek and [I] kept focusing on what seemed an awfully big mountain over in Brush Creek."

The mountain, Baldy, was only about eight miles southwest of Aspen. He flew over it, studied a U.S. Geological Survey map of the area, and compared its site, size and slope with both Aspen Mountain and Aspen Highlands. He also went up the mountain several times on skis with climbing skins. Several things became clear: (1) Baldy was a mountain of enormous promise, (2) profitable development depended on Janss buying all the land at the upper end of the Brush Creek Valley, and (3) if word of Janss's intentions got out, the price of the land would skyrocket.

Pitcher and the Janss boys hired a real estate broker to bargain for the key ranch at the base of Baldy. He got it for $80,000. To create the impression that they were merely ranchers, they imported steers from the California feed lot to run on their new Brush Creek ranch and on Pitcher's Woody Creek ranch. They ultimately acquired all the land they needed at agricultural rather than development prices.

Janss, Pitcher, Thomas and the other puritan playboys were always fit, frequently handsome, usually rich and inevitably arrogant. Some bore noble American names and some merely looked worthy of great names and fortunes. They often had as much or more money than Aspen's richer citizens, and they were usually as freewheeling as the ski bums. Their interest in fashion, their passion for being "in," and their ability to go in several directions at once worked on Aspen like a fresh but contrary wind. They had a boundless interest in the present. Aspen was suspicious of them, but it could not resist them because they always acted with grace. They looked like all the good guys in all the movies.

IN THE SPRING OF 1958 Thornton Wilder drove into Aspen in a smart gray Thunderbird. The town, he said, looked wonderful. He had always liked it. If it had a good library, he could imagine retiring there, he said. But he had come to resign from the board of the Institute because he didn't much like board work, and in any case, he wasn't sure that the effort to turn businessmen into philosophers was worth the effort. "Avoid the rich, shun them," he said to a group of people in the Jerome bar one afternoon.

He spent much of his week in Aspen in the Jerome bar. He liked to drink and he liked to talk, and he liked the Jerome because the late afternoon light was good there, the drinks were generous, the old bar had nothing of the cocktail lounge about it, and from time to time interesting people came in. Besides, he said, it was very convenient to his room, pointing to the bar ceiling and smiling. Wilder was invited everywhere, to small dinner parties and huge cocktail parties. Aspen went all out for him, but he refused most of the invitations and just drifted around town. He liked Newt's, a resolutely plain western bar where the cowboys gathered to drink away their disappointments. He said they were wiser than all of the Institute scholars and told wonderful profane stories.

He said that a lot of fools had gathered in Aspen, and though fools do foolish things, the place itself seemed as sound as it was in 1949. When Wilder left Aspen, he had resigned from the Institute's board, but he had simultaneously accepted a position on its advisory committee. Though he could not quite accept the Institute's lofty goals, he could not bring himself to entirely disavow them either. As he drove off, he waved and said he would return, but he never came to Aspen again.

IN THE FIFTIES, as "massness" spread across America like a noxious fog, Aspen shone like a gallant beacon. It was the product of a time warp, and that time warp had been artfully improved until it had become the product. America came to Aspen in the way that people travel across the country to see houses in which they were once young and happy. Those houses often seem too small or too shabby or at odds with our nostalgia for them; but Aspen did not disappoint America.

It pranced and stepped high and light and seemed full of juices that had dried up elsewhere in America. It was still young, fresh and sassy in a mean, tired time. The nation was hard at work, but play was the first principle in Aspen. The nation had got dull and slow, but Aspen was still moving fast and easy. The nation was caught up in "togetherness," but Aspen celebrated the individual. Long before it was fashionable, ME was elevated over US, over YOU, over THEM. In a gray-flannel buttoned-up nation, Aspen residents went about in Levi's and sneakers. Getting ahead was the American imperative; living well—meaning living with a minimum of money, responsibility and burdens, and a maximum of style and zest—was the Aspen imperative. Aspen gave new meaning to that ancient Spanish proverb: Living well is the best revenge.

What was going on in Aspen looked like heresy or madness to much of America, but it looked like fun to the influential minority that had the time and money to indulge in art and sport. As the fifties wound down, that minority grew. Aspen was as different from the rest of America as Huckleberry Finn is different from Babbitt. Vance Packard's best seller *The Status Seekers* defined a slicker, faster breed of Babbitt that was taking over the nation. In Aspen, however, no one spoke of "status."

The national mood was strident. The most popular songs of 1959 were "He's Got the Whole World in His Hands," "Everything's Coming Up Roses," "The Sound of Music" and "High Hopes." These songs reflected a national need for good news in a time that was full of bad news. Steelworkers and longshoremen went out on long strikes that ended only when President Eisenhower invoked the Taft-Hartley Act and ordered the men back to work. Unemployment was climbing. Statistics showed that 1.25 million Americans had been killed in automobile accidents over the decade—more than all the dead in all the wars in which America participated. C. Wright Mills, a leading sociologist, wrote a book called *The Causes of World War III* that was not flattering to America. The nation's first moon rocket fell many miles short of the moon. The beat generation, which found much to deplore and nothing to love in America, spread out of California and across America. In Aspen, there were no strikes, no unemployment, and there were no beatniks.

As America faltered, Aspen's confidence grew. The town seemed the one true oasis. Hubris is sometimes its own reward—in people and in places.

7⌃
Coming Unstuck

A S ORDER EMERGES out of chaos, so chaos emerges out of order.

On April 13, 1960 Walter Paepcke died, a victim of cancer. He devoted the last months of his life to putting his enterprises in order, but his death itself triggered an era of disorder for Aspen. The town reeled when he died, but it did not pause. Too much was happening. Everything, including its own resistence to the mainstream, conspired to move Aspen into the spotlight and hold it there.

The 1960 winter Olympics were held in Squaw Valley, California, and were televised nationally. The speed, glamour and excitement of skiing bewitched thousands of affluent Americans who had become increasingly restless. After the war, they moved from the cities to the suburbs, which were meant to be the ideal environment, combining the best of city life with the best of country life to make the much-trumpeted "good life." Too often, however, the suburbs combined the provincialism of the country with the anomie of the city. After a decade in these netherlands, suburbanites went looking for something more or something else. Travel calmed the itch, satisfied the old American appetite for the new and the novel. Trips and places visited were racked up in the way old soldiers add up citations and medals. Experiences of the right sort conferred a kind of status, and it was clear after Squaw Valley that skiing was experience of the right sort. The new ski equipment was sleek, lightweight and easy to use. Ski clothes were finally stylish and flattering. Attired in Willy Bogner's stretch pants and quilted parkas, identified by the discreet "B" on the zipper, one did not even have to ski to look like a pro.

The quest of this new breed of pioneer was not for rich farmland or even for silver or gold, but for good times and new places that bore no resemblance to the old home town. Small towns were dull and poor. Big cities were dirty and dangerous. Suburbs were bland and boring. The resort was the perfect 1960s environment—different, even exotic, certainly amusing—and the elite and chic ski resort was the perfect resort. Aspen was not only the largest ski resort in America, it was also the most original, exciting and sophisticated, but somehow, as visitors repeated with wonder, unspoiled.

Affluent America, with its great and careless energy, its boundless confidence, its vaulting ambitions, its endless need for new things, came to Aspen to visit, to live and to develop. The town was booming, and it was beset. Walter Paepcke was gone, and no one could tell the residents what to do, how to handle the town, what to think about its new popularity. Almost overnight, skiing had been transformed from an adventure to an industry. When it was an adventure, its imperatives were fast slopes, practical gear and excellence. When it became an industry, its imperatives were ever-enlarging numbers of skiers on the slopes, fashionable gear and profit.

The Aspen Skiing Corporation emphatically noted the transformation when it raised the rate of resident chil-

dren's lift tickets from 75 cents to $2. From the time that
Aspen Mountain had opened, it had been a kind of absolute democracy for children. Virtually every child in
Aspen could afford the 75-cent ticket, but the $2 fee
would effectively bar many of them from the mountain.

Several upset mothers attempted to persuade the directors of the Skiing Corporation to rescind the rate
increase, but were unable to do so. Directors said that
the Corporation was not a philanthropic organization
but a business, and that the local children skied too fast,
showed off and were generally rude to visitors. The
women organized a Mother's March through downtown
Aspen that climaxed with the burning of an effigy, la-
belled "D. R. C. Hodges." The march was made by more
children than mothers. They carried rude placards.
Bugsy Barnard turned up in a smart wool dress, carrying
a sign reading "World's Greatest Motha." The increase
ultimately held because D. R. C. Brown favored it, and
what Brown favored, he usually got.

David Robinson Crockett Brown, who succeeded
Denver lawyer William Hodges as the president of the
Aspen Skiing Corporation, had considerable clout, and
he used it. Brown was the son of one of the few Aspen
pioneers who had not only survived the bad times but
prospered. Until his death in 1930 the senior Brown was
the most powerful man in Aspen, counting among his
extensive holdings the light and power companies. As a
verse from the time shows, he was not universally admired:

> Now look at our little city, and its case with
> David Brown.
> He raised the light bill all at once to keep the
> miners down.

Now this isn't elegant language, no sir, upon
your soul.
But David got the doughnut and the city gets
the hole.

Like his father, D. R. C. Brown almost always got the
doughnut. Thin, balding, fine-featured, Brown looks like
the clerk his father once was, but he behaves like the
baron his father became. His voice has a raspy edge, an
adolescent pitch. He is shy at parties, and not particularly accomplished at public speaking. Although he
owned some of the mining claims that became part of
the Skiing Corporation's holdings, he was not a major
stockholder. His second wife, Ruth Humphreys, is heiress to a great Colorado fortune and one of the richest
women in the state. They keep a small house in Aspen
but live on a large ranch down the valley in Carbondale.
When Brown became president of the Skiing Corporation, he began to run it as if his life were at stake and
exerted the kind of one-man control that has all but
vanished in the upper reaches of American business.

The hike in lift ticket rates for resident children was
only the first in an endless round of increases. Brown said
often that not only did residents not deserve special
privileges, they were also unwelcome on Aspen Mountain. As not everyone could afford to drive a Cadillac, he
remarked, not everyone could afford to ski in Aspen. He
would tolerate no "interference" from local, state or federal officials in the workings of the Skiing Corporation.
Its first responsibility was to its stockholders.

Businessman Brown was as parochial as businessman
Paepcke had been catholic in his views, but he did ex-
tend part of Paepcke's notion. If the business of Aspen
was happiness, then the business of happiness should be

profitable. Brown obviously saw nothing intrinsically worthy in Aspen's small scale. He dreamed not of "the whole man" but of profits. His swift ascent in Aspen in the 1960s seemed at once a renunciation of Paepcke's vision, and a confirmation of the paternalistic tradition he had initiated there.

AS THE SIXTIES BEGAN, America was doing the twist, on the dance floor and in life. Bad news was epidemic. Russia snared an American U2 spy plane, and put its pilot on trial. Freedom Riders working to integrate the South were beaten by bigots. Adolph Eichmann, a Nazi war criminal, was caught and put on trial, and unspeakable acts were made public. *Psycho,* a Hitchcock master-piece, featured blood and gore. Hemingway shot himself in the mouth, a victim of what he himself had earlier described as "a failure of nerve." J. D. Salinger chroni-cled the manic, guilt-ridden lives of the Glass family. Joseph Heller's novel *Catch-22* said that life was a game no one could win. Vance Packard indicted Americans as *The Waste Makers.* Eighty-five million households had TV sets; and a TV hero, Charles Van Doren, a handsome young professor, was accused of cheating on a game show. Emily Post, the mistress of good manners, died.

But a handsome young hero, John Kennedy, came ri-ding out of Boston, narrowly defeated perennial bad guy Richard M. Nixon, and immediately cheered up the na-tion. He was different from all the Presidents who had gone before. He was young, handsome, rich, witty and Catholic. His optimism and eloquence and style engaged us as no President since Franklin D. Roosevelt had. Kennedy seemed to epitomize the best in us. America was, in his words, "The New Frontier," brand-new again, vigorous, promising, accessible to everyone, susceptible to the wildest dreams. The bright new President was himself the leading dreamer, and he dreamed of patriots, brotherhood, prosperity and men on the moon.

From the moment the continent was discovered, men were drawn irresistibly to its frontier, its farthermost edge. That edge stayed ahead of them all the way— through Pennsylvania, Ohio, Indiana, Nebraska, all the way to the Pacific. Once there, America turned around and went in search of other frontiers: industrial supremacy, wealth, power, truth, beauty. In the same way, people moved from farms to cities to suburbs to resorts, seeking more. When Kennedy announced the New Frontier, after the Depression, World War II and fifteen years of solemn greed, the lid blew off again. There were as many frontiers to be sought as there were people to seek them. Alert composed men whirled higher and higher into outer space, while others sought new frontiers inside their heads with the help of drugs. Business had never been better, and neither had pleasure.

Born late, America had no time to mature before the Industrial Revolution that had begun to spread across the world in 1770 overtook it. The reasons for the country's creation were at odds with the needs of industrialism, so they fell by the wayside. In 1876 the nation's centennial celebration focused on its industrial and commercial achievements. Philosophical and political concerns were beside the point. Business boomed and busted, wars were fought and won, and it became clear after World War II that the reasons for the wars were as cloudy as the reasons for the country. It all came home during the Bay of Pigs fiasco, when the CIA backed an invasion of Cuba by anti-Castro forces. America seemed no longer to understand itself or its place in the world. But Kennedy did an unprecedented thing: he said it was his fault, this Caribbean idiocy. In fact, the plan had been set in motion during the Eisenhower years. But the Presidential confession was a kind of catharsis for the nation. It cleared the air and let America get on with it.

Challenging the nation again and again, Kennedy said we were prosperous enough to do everything. It was time for the arts and sciences to flourish, for the Bill of Rights to be finally affirmed, for democracy to proceed. He was a consummate politician and not nearly as adventurous as he looked, but his timing was exquisite. The country was ready to be moved and he moved it. It did not really matter that he moved it more by rhetoric and personal example than by actions, because it was moving. It was, for a while, a promising time. It was also tumultuous and angry. Institutions were questioned, sometimes savagely examined. People took to the streets, and sometimes battled. Only a hopeful people are capable of rebellion, and many people were suddenly hopeful. The assaults on the status quo were myriad and occasionally violent. Blacks and other minorities wanted at last what had been denied them too long. Young people were in open revolt. Blue-collar workers were the new conservatives. Music, clothes and attitudes were all changing in fundamental ways. The Beatles, four young men from Liverpool, England, were new American folk heroes.

There were new villains, such as big business, and there were new causes: the environment, liberation, civil rights, love. Born in the American Revolution but shaped by the Industrial Revolution, America seemed to be trying to unmake itself, to be reborn in the 1960s.

John Kennedy opened up the country. He turned its imagination back on, stirred it, and then he was killed. In 1960, 49 percent of the people voted for him. After he died, 65 percent claimed to have voted for him. The country mourned him, but his death only moved it faster.

In challenging Americans to do all the things they had left undone and to do things no people had done before, Kennedy had suggested that the sixties were to be years of unprecedented tests. After his death, the tests got mean. In the three years he was in the White House, about 16,000 American soldiers were sent to Vietnam to help the pro-American regime battle Communist insurgents. This "assistance" became a war soon after he died. From the moment he took office the day Kennedy was assassinated through his 1964 battle with Senator Barry Goldwater for the White House, Lyndon Johnson promised to wind the war down. Goldwater vowed to send enough men, planes and bombs to Vietnam to win. Johnson was elected to his first full term by a landslide and escalated the war beyond even Goldwater's scenario. He pushed vital civil rights legislation through Congress in the name of the dead President, but his heart was in Vietnam. In his Great Society, which had replaced the New Frontier, everything was possible. We could afford guns and butter, Johnson said. But the Great Society was no sooner named than it began to unravel.

Two hundred thousand people went to Washington in behalf of civil rights and heard Dr. Martin Luther King, Jr., describe his dream. Thousands of other people marched to protest the war. Young men were burning their draft cards, going to jail or leaving the country rather than join the army. Pro-war zealots battled antiwar demonstrators in the streets. More men, more arms, more money were committed to Vietnam. America had never lost a war, but it seemed to be losing to a ragtag band of insurgents in a country few Americans had ever heard of. It was at war with itself, too, and losing.

Martin Luther King won the Nobel Peace Prize. Bob Dylan's "Blowin' in the Wind" was a new national anthem. Families divided over the war, civil rights, sexual freedom. It was a fast, fraught time. America did the Watusi, Frug, Monkey and Funky Chicken; read Ken Kesey's *One Flew over the Cuckoo's Nest,* which suggested America was a madhouse; believed Andy Warhol when he said Campbell's soup cans were art, and Stanley Kubrick when he showed in *Dr. Strangelove* how the world would end. Pop went the art, bang went the world.

America had only flirted with Aspen during the fifties. The town was like the carefree girl at the dull party—intriguing, but dangerous in some way. In the sixties the love affair began in earnest, because America had changed radically and Aspen hadn't changed at all.

Aspen was as beautifully situated as any town in America. It boasted tennis courts in bubbles, concert masters in the tent, small cold lakes at the end of long dusty trails, movie stars on the chairlifts. There were no angry blacks, no clumsy ethnics, no rude blue-collar workers, no factories or skyscrapers full of automatons, no billboards or neon to remind one of vile commerce. One might have thought that the revolution had already taken place in Aspen, The Big Questions been resolved, and everyone was now living happily ever after. In fact, the revolution never got to Aspen. The town remained out of time, an innocent frolicking up there in the high country. The fun and games went on unabated.

Aspen residents said no, I won't go to war or to work or anyplace I don't want to go. The cities were burning, but Aspen was building. A social critic, having been to the Institute, wondered whether "life on the mountaintop" taught anything about life. Aspen protested, noting that rapacious developers had the mountaintop in their sights and were threatening to "overdevelop" it. While "war" and "bigotry" were dirty words to many Americans, "development" and "growth" were the dirty words in Aspen.

Hubris nourished Aspen during the long lonesome decades between the silver bust and the ski boom. Hubris was implicit in Walter Paepcke's plan to create a town that celebrated Goethe, powder runs, music, lectures and the most benign sort of rebellion, a town that said no more often than yes to the times. It was a measure of the enduring hubris of Aspen that it thought it could remain out of time in the volatile sixties. It was prepared for none of the assaults on it, benign or otherwise. We knew everything about America, and therefore nothing.

TOURISTS CAME to Aspen in increasing numbers, and as new businessmen moved in, neo-beatniks dropped off the road to settle there. They didn't consider themselves residents of anywhere. They had given up on America and wandered the underground circuit from Greenwich Village to Big Sur to Aspen. They cared nothing for politics, only for literature and life. One of these intellectual itinerants, Paul Semonin, had come to the new underground Aspen by way of Kentucky, Yale and Puerto Rico. He was working as a waiter while writing a book, *The Collected Thoughts of a Tramp Thinker.* Semonin was not in residence when Hunter S. Thompson, an old friend from Kentucky, arrived in town. Thompson appeared on my doorstep one bleak fall night in 1960, having just driven a car full of bamboo bird cages from San Francisco to Aspen nonstop. He was exhausted and angry. On his way from Big Sur to Louisville, he contracted to drive the car to Aspen for $50—"to see Semonin's dream," he said. He was traveling with a gentle, anxious Doberman named Agar and a large jug of red wine. We took the car to its owner, a woman who ran an Aspen interior design shop. She was playing bridge. She invited us in, gave us drinks, and went back to the bridge table. Thompson wanted his $50 and wanted to be out of there. The woman suggested he relax until the game was over. Thompson stared bleakly at the players for a while and finally said, "Jesus, Semonin's dream looks just like the God damn Louisville Country Club."

In the morning, after seeing Semonin's cabin on Aspen Mountain, he spent his $50 on a train ticket and headed home, stone broke. A week later, I got a letter from him. Enclosed was his lucky silver dollar. He said, "I would never give away a paper dollar, but a solid one given at the appropriate time and place brings extreme luck. And living the way I do, I figure I need extreme luck."

When I met him, Thompson was in his mid-twenties and had already been fired by the Air Force because he turned all of his G.I. trousers into Bermuda shorts and took a full-time job as a sportswriter for a local newspaper. He had been fired by a New York state daily for kicking in the candy machine; and fired by *Time* magazine for his inability to engage successfully in committee journalism. He'd also bummed around the Caribbean, where he'd begun a novel, *Rum Diary*. Now he was on his way to Rio to write for the *National Observer*.

Thompson is tall, graceful and strong like an athlete, but he is pale-faced. His skin is fine, almost translucent and very smooth. Sometimes there are blue shadows around his eyes. His face in repose is like a mask. It gives away nothing. But he has the eyes, the smile of a rogue.

His eyes and his smile contain more mischief than any one person should have. He is one of those men who get the attention of the world and keep it.

When Semonin got back and heard of Thompson's arrival and abrupt departure, of his vision of Aspen as the Louisville Country Club, he only smiled and said, "He'll be back."

8^

The Clean Sweep

H ARALD "SHORTY" PABST, beer baron, rancher, Institute trustee and Aspen Skiing Corporation director, was the first man to grab for Paepkcke's throne. There were superficial similarities. Both came from the Midwest and were of German stock. Like Paepcke, Pabst had lived in the valley for a number of years, had plenty of money and time and a genuine interest in the community. He'd even worked with Paepcke on some Institute projects. But Paepcke was a sophisticated businessman who had succeeded in the marketplace before moving on to the groves of academe. Pabst was a rich man, untested in either business or scholarship. Paepcke had a subtle ironic view of life. Pabst was a righteous simple man who tended to see everything as black or white.

Tall, boyish even in middle age, Pabst looked like a cowboy, and, like his friend D. R. C. Brown, he always expected to have his own way. He chose politics, not business or culture, as his vehicle in Aspen, and almost immediately managed to make politics as noisy, acrimonious and aggressive as it had always been in other places.

In 1962 Pabst assembled the "Clean Sweep" ticket with himself as mayoral candidate, Bugsy Barnard, two other newcomers and a young native as council candidates. Like most righteous men, Pabst was given to overstatement. The "Clean Sweep" slogan suggested that the incumbents were rascals who must be got out of city hall. In fact they were simply rather dull men doing the best they could in a hectic time. Pabst pledged a more aggressive stance, a cranking up of the civic machinery. It was another rejection of Paepcke's philosophy and paralleled politically what Brown was doing in business.

The incumbents knew little of politics or campaigning. Their ads merely said that votes for them would be appreciated, while the "Clean Sweep" campaign was a blitzkreig of plans and promises. It was the first time that newer residents had tried to work their will on Aspen politically, and they won easily. Politics immediately became the dominant game in the valley. When Mayor Pabst installed himself in Pioneer Park, which the Paepckes had made into Aspen's most elegant house, it was said that he saw Aspen more as a kind of principality to be ruled than a community to be governed.

The new mayor immediately ordered enlargements and improvements in everything from the electric system to publicity and promotion. Streets would be paved. A sewer system would be built. A city manager was hired. When Pabst stated flatly that Aspen did not want "the hot dog crowd," the town's ersatz egalitarians were horrified, even though Aspen has legislated against the average man and for the elite from 1945 to the present. The character of the elite has varied through the years, but the thrust of the legislation has been constant. As Pabst ordered more and more embellishments and the city budget escalated, it became clear that he saw his power as absolute. His most outspoken opponent was Barnard. Their battle began when Barnard accused

Pabst of using his office to promote the interests of the Institute over the interests of the town. In the ensuing feud, the Aspen political style took shape—attack, counterattack, no holds barred, anything goes.

FOR AN INCREASING NUMBER of Americans, Aspen became one of those places that one had to visit. Those people who came to test themselves physically and intellectually in the high country were outnumbered in the sixties by adventurers in search of prestigious experiences. Shrunken heads, scalps on a belt, notches on the gun, tiger heads on the wall. The Adler lecture, the Primrose performance, the powder on the back of Bell, a sighting of Eric Sevareid or James "Matt Dillon" Arness.

Aspen's dazzling setting, its freewheeling style, its originality, its clever mix of art and sport made it singularly desirable. Because it was out of step, it was in vogue. Americans—many of them anyway—had grown tired of the country they had made. This new rebellious America was for them not only uncomfortable, it was itself proof of generations of mistakes and lapses. America was full of rebels now, but Aspen's rebels were . . . nice. They were healthy. They enjoyed sports and art, and had no interest at all in rousing the rabble. But as affluent America adopted Aspen, Aspen residents debated the merits of affluence.

Out-of-town developers were the first people to openly challenge the assumptions that Aspen was somehow beyond heavyweight commerce, and that the small scale and spaciousness of the town were inviolate; and for several years, they built while residents merely argued with each other. The sense of community that had flourished during Paepcke's time had begun to erode. To the developers, Aspen was merely a rich market, an ideal site for a new resort phenomenon: the condominium. Few residents even knew what a condominium was, and no one knew what to think of them. As they watched the buildings go up, some residents wanted to stop the invaders in their tracks by whatever means necessary, and some simply mourned the passing of serene times. Some believed they could somehow orchestrate the boom, and some rushed to enlist on the side of the invaders. With the town in fundamental disarray, this new breed of prospector bent on mining money took over Aspen as easily as the miners had taken over the valley eighty years before.

Large new buildings squeezed out small houses; old neighborhoods were obilterated. Town and mountain were divided as ranks of condominiums rose like a wall between them. Where there had been spaciousness and long views, one now found clutter and fragmented vistas. Giant kitsch-Swiss chalets, ersatz-Bauhaus boxes and ponderous edifices of timber and stone began to dominate the townscape. The small ski lodge was suddenly an anachronism.

Visitors could not understand the residents' rage and confusion. The town, by any standards, was still clean, airy and serene. The commercial blight that had begun to creep beyond the cities and into the suburbs had not come even close to Aspen. This, visitors said, is paradise.

This, residents replied, used to be paradise. The building boom multiplied the number of available tourist beds, and attracted new residents and businesses. It forced up the cost of living and diminished residential housing. "Condominiumization" was a cold name for a cold process. Many of the younger residents who had lived in midtown Aspen on the upper floors of business buildings were ousted by owners who refurbished the apartments and sold them as condominiums to part-time residents for very fancy prices. As transients captured the heart of Aspen, residents were exiled to the hinterlands. The price of land and houses began to rise rapidly. There were, it seemed, an infinite number of people who wanted vacation digs in Aspen, and for whom price was no object. In 1963 the price of the average condominium was $22,000 and rising fast. By the end of the 1960s the price was over $100,000 and still rising.

Aspen was becoming, in the words of one resident, "a cash register." Much of the money that came in went right out again. The developers and many of the contractors played hit and run—built, sold and moved on. Condominium owners were virtually all out-of-towners and enjoyed tax breaks that resident homeowners were denied. One could buy a condominium, use it several times a year, rent it short-term for the rest of the year, apply the rental income to the purchase price, and write off most expenses courtesy of the IRS while the apartment appreciated rapidly in value. The profits that accrued in the buying and selling went to absentee owners, while the financial and social costs were borne by residents.

Absentee owners and developers wanted and got all of the conveniences and amenities they were accustomed to back in Chicago or Dallas or Kansas City. City and county budgets soared as roads and sewers, municipally owned water and electric departments, law enforcement and social service agencies enlarged. Booming growth in the private sector triggered bureaucratic explosions in city hall and the county courthouse. Crime, air pollution and heavy traffic were seen in Aspen for the first time.

The 1955 zoning ordinance had been designed pri-

marily to maintain a certain order in a placid time, and
it was wholly inadequate in the face of the 1960s real
estate rush. City and county officials fudged; most had no
stomach for abridging individual rights for something as
amorphous as "the public good," and some present and
past officials were participating in the boom. Barnard
had been buying and selling land and houses for several
years. Former mayor Mike Garish sold the old family
plot to a supermarket owner and moved his house across
the river into a less promising neighborhood. County
Commissioner Orest Gerbaz sold a piece of his ranch to
some New York investors who turned it into a trailer
court. A nephew of Mayor Pabst's built a large and luxurious condominium complex near the bottom of the
mountain. There was nothing illegal about such transac-
tions, but the town divided over them. Worms have
somehow got into the apple, we said, and some of those
worms are residents. Better that we keep the apple for
our own, others said. Worms are worms, we replied, and
they must all be dealt with rudely. But none of us acted.

In the 1880s and early 1890s, silver had been Aspen's
principal commodity. In the late 1940s and 1950s, culture and snow had been sold, though very chastely. In
the 1960s the place itself was for sale. Our notion of
Aspen as a place with very particular imperatives and
rewards was being challenged. Both the condominium
boom and the newly aggressive posture of the Chamber
of Commerce, which had begun spending tax money as
well as business contributions on a national promotion
and advertising campaign, demonstrated a shift from
reverence for the place to a desire to exploit it.

The paving of fourteen blocks of downtown Aspen
looked like the beginning of the end to some residents.
Unpaved streets had been not only adequate but cher-

ished by residents and visiting eccentrics who found some vestigial virtue in the dust and bumps. They were proof after all that Aspen had not succumbed with the rest of America to the primitive worship of the automobile. Dour prophets said that the paved streets were proof of our capitulation to commercial interests. It can only end badly now, they said.

There was another more ominous portent. For the first time in seventy years, the Hotel Jerome was closed. The directors of the Aspen Institute, holder of the lease, explained that the Institute was in the conference business, not the hotel business. They wanted to sell. But though residents saw this as one more sign of the imminent demise of the town, the closing of the Jerome actually told more about the alteration of the Institute.

WALTER PAEPCKE'S hand-picked successor was Robert O. Anderson. His background was remarkably similar to Paepcke's, but he used it quite differently. The son of a banker specializing in oil, Anderson, like Paepcke, grew up in Chicago. He had a similar classical education, and began his business career with a small edge. He graduated from the University of Chicago during the reign of Paepcke's ally Hutchins, and moved to New Mexico with the stated intention of making enough money by the time he was forty to live as he wished. As it turned out, he became the country's single largest landholder, one of its most successful independent oilmen and an arts patron. He has, over time, enjoyed all of the prerogatives of wealth except leisure. On a fishing trip to Aspen in 1953, he met Paepcke and became the Institute's principal benefactor. He was made its president and after Paepcke's death, its chairman.

Anderson has pumped money into the Institute since

1953; he's also donated land and buildings to the Aspen Historical Society and to the Music Associates of Aspen. His devotion to Aspen's cultural institutions in general and the Institute in particular has been abiding. But while Paepcke saw the Institute and Aspen as synonymous and regarded the Institute as an end in itself, Anderson has seen the two as separate and seems to see the Institute as a means. Soon after Paepcke died, Anderson began to move the Institute into that vague but powerful international community of scholars, businessmen and politicians called the Establishment. In 1962 Bob Craig was eased out of the Institute and replaced by Alvin C. Eurich, a one-time Ford Foundation official.

Herbert Bayer went to work for Anderson after Paepcke's death. One of his first projects was the restoration of a lovely old Spanish chapel on one of Anderson's ranches. Another was designing the Paepcke Auditorium on the Institute campus. Unlike Bayer's previous buildings in Aspen, the auditorium was large, bold, emphatic. If in conversation he mourned the passing of the small Victorian oasis he had helped restore, his work exemplified new times and new imperatives.

The replacement of local boy Craig with Eurich, the increasing number of national leaders who came to the Institute and the enlargement of its programs all suggested that the Institute was taking a new tack.

In the increasingly tumultuous sixties in Aspen, residents looked in vain to the Institute for leadership and direction. Early on, Anderson had said that he did not intend to play Paepcke's role in Aspen, either as philosophical or financial Godfather. For one thing, he said, Paepcke had been hurt by occasional dust-ups with townspeople. For another, Anderson had many other enterprises in other places.

Paepcke had spent most of the year in Aspen. Anderson came and went, staying for a day or a week at a time. Eurich spent more and more time in the Institute's new New York offices. Both men remained aloof from the turmoil in Aspen. As America came into the valley, the Institute left it—philosophically if not physically.

The Aspen Music Festival and School, though it had split with Paepcke in 1954, carried his vision faithfully into the 1960s. Courtlandt Barnes, the Festival chairman, focused almost wholly on the Festival. Like Paepcke, he believed that small scale was an ingredient of excellence. This avid concertgoer became an adept concert manager. While everything around it burgeoned, the Festival remained constant, relying on the power of art to find an audience. From time to time, there were arguments between the musicians and the trustees, but the musicians usually prevailed, and so the Festival stayed on course, achieving the kind of quiet renown Paepcke had wanted for the place itself.

Ironically, as Walter Paepcke's enterprises flourished, each in its own fashion, his widow was shoved aside. Perhaps the only thing Elizabeth Paepcke was less prepared for than her husband's early death was her subsequent uncivil treatment in Aspen. As her husband's vision faded, her counsel was pointedly ignored by Anderson and his Institute associates and by most townspeople. The king was dead, and the continued presence of the queen was bothersome, for she reminded us of our obligations to the kingdom. But she would not go away.

She continued to spend much time in her Aspen house, and she emerged from a time of mourning ready to do battle for those things in Aspen that she valued. There was steel in her now. Whenever and wherever she could, she reminded people of their obligation to preserve what was good and oppose what was bad. No one listened. But she refused to give up, refused to go into voluntary exile, and refused to be silent.

Her husband had brought Aspen back to life. He had given it a reason for being, and built a solid economic base for it, and then he had died. Aspen's natural beauty was intact, its spacious and sturdy townscape had been restored, its population was energetic and talented. It was the best of all possible worlds, but it was coming unstuck. That is what Elizabeth Paepcke saw and that is what she said.

Walter Paepcke's legacy to Aspen was enormous: the Aspen Institute, the Aspen Music Festival and School, the International Design Conference in Aspen, the Aspen Skiing Corporation, and such services as Aspen Airways. But Elizabeth Paepcke's challenge was even more enormous. You have inherited Aspen, she said, and you must cherish it, build on my husband's accomplishments. To put it baldly, she told us to grow up and get on with it. But her challenge went unheard, even unremarked as the residents searched for another Big Daddy.

HUNTER THOMPSON and his wife Sandy moved to Aspen in the late summer of 1963. They took a small house on eleven acres in Woody Creek. The coincidence of their arrival with Dick Gibson's jazz party demonstrated that the town, and we ourselves, were still capable of a little preposterousness.

The jazz party and the recently reopened Jerome were made for each other. Gibson had missed jazz when he moved to Denver from New York. Being a man of exquisite inclinations, he searched Colorado for a hall, found the Jerome, invited twenty jazzmen and several hundred paying guests at $25 each to Aspen for a week-end.

It was a cool gray day, but the Jerome dining room was full of light. The audience wore expensive country clothes—tweeds, flannels, cashmere. Everyone was easy, smiled, drank. The music began. The players jammed in endless combinations and mixes. Trios, quartets, piano duets, reed battles, drum and bass skirmishes. They played sweet and hot and sad. Everyone smiled, kept time with feet, hands, heads, yelled MORE after every number, and there was more.

Trombonist Cutty Cutshall, a tall shambling man with waxy skin and black hair, looked too tired to stand up, but made his horn sigh and growl and roar. Piano man Teddy Wilson, small and dapper, with the nose of a hawk and the eyes of a saint, barely moved, but his fingers traveled eons on the keyboard. Major Holley growled with his bass, got so close to it that one could hardly tell which was the instrument and which the player.

The music stopped about seven o'clock. Players and listeners trailed away, still jamming a little, and returned at nine, men in dinner jackets, women in pale silk dresses. It was a different room, dim, intimate, but the music remained triumphant.

Dick Gibson had the echo of a Deep South accent, the height and bulk of a football player, and the smile of an angel. He was a very big businessman who liked to sing with jazzmen. His favorite song begins, "Nobody loves you when you're down and out. . . ." He grinned like a boy when he sang it.

Clarinetist Edmund Hall had the face of a pharoah, with enormous, exhausted eyes. He tilted his head back, closed those eyes, and blew a fine true line that soared, dipped, took hold of the air and hung there. Wild Bill

Davison, slick-haired, tightly packed, with a boyish bounce, was the funny man—sassy, jokey, gleaming with fun. Gibson gave him an Old West trophy, a six-shooter. The next morning he leaned out of his hotel window, waved the gun and shot it, surprising himself and everyone in the vicinity. He played a rowdy, tailgate cornet, and seemed all energy and air.

The music ended at 2:00 A.M. We left the premises slowly, silently, all used up.

The next morning there were Bloody Marys on every table. We sat quietly, reverent with exhaustion. The players were freshly shaved, a bit too glittery in the eye. Their hair was still damp from the shower, their white shirts crisp, their hands pink and clean as surgeons' hands, but in a few minutes they were easy as a summer afternoon.

Edmund Hall played with Freddie Fisher. The tall elegant black king, the short grizzled philosopher. When they were done, Fisher's smile encompassed the universe.

Sutton. Ralph Sutton touched the piano and it went all fleet and crystal. He contained orchestras in his hands, more chords and notes than ever existed before. It was impossible not to smile when he played. One heard everything one wanted to hear and more, things one had been waiting to hear forever, and all the while he smiled in a tight, secret and ironic way. He is a direct descendant of Fats Waller, but he was tall, wore tweed coats, sneakers, horn-rimmed glasses and did not look like a piano man at all.

Late Sunday afternoon it was over. There wasn't anything more. The musicians climbed limp and sleepy onto a bus. We drifted away from the hotel too, but humming, jangling gently, looser and lighter than before. I had been to the heart of the matter and decided to stay there. But I didn't. I drifted on the Aspen tides with everyone else.

People said the valley itself was under siege, the air was rancorous, but Thompson, Semonin and I stayed out of the struggle and on the sidelines. We reasoned that we were neither businessmen nor politicians, and they had charge of the place. None of us had actively supported the "Clean Sweep" ticket, and we didn't much like Pabst, but we thought it was interesting and perhaps healthy that newcomers were taking over city hall. They were more like us than the old-timers and therefore would cherish the place as we did. Of course, in those days, we still believed in progress.

9^
Alarums and Incursions

I HEARD IT FROM Patsy Forbes, who heard it from Mrs. Earl Hose, a dressmaker. Mrs. Forbes called to check on some alterations. Mrs. Hose said, "The President's been shot." I went home and sat in front of my television set in the way that people sit in front of altars. He died. I went downtown. Everyone was silent, dazed, dark. I saw Sunny Anderson, who owned a restaurant. I said, "Are you going to open tonight?" I couldn't think of anything else to say. She shook her head as if she were trying to make sense out of the question. Finally she said, "Sometimes you just have to stop, don't you?" I nodded and went home. The days were mean as crows.

The momentum of the sixties was neither slowed nor diverted. America and Aspen barreled right along, brokenhearted but still bold and brassy.

Billy Janss talked a lot about Thoreau, whose works he had discovered in an Aspen Institute seminar. He also talked about his new ski area, Snowmass-at-Aspen (later Snowmass Resort). Janss's version of Walden Pond wasn't particularly Thoreauvian.

Janss's man in Aspen, Kingsbury Pitcher, had traveled endlessly up and down and across Baldy on an old Army weasel, "one of the most treacherous vehicles ever conceived." He chose sites for runs, noted the location of wide bowls, planned lift routes, but was dealt out abruptly when Janss turned the design and development of the mountain over to the Aspen Skiing Corporation. It would, after all, pay for the privilege and was expert in these matters. With its acquisition of Baldy, the Skiing Corporation, which had already bought Buttermilk from Pfeifer, was back on top. Almost simultaneously Janss Investment sold a half-interest in the land at the base of the mountain to the American Cement Corporation. Together, Janss announced, they would build a ski town complete with condominiums, houses, restaurants, shops and businesses.

In 1964 the U.S. Forest Service approved the Janss plan for West Village. The first phase was to be a $75 million development at the head of Brush Creek, along with what the Skiing Corporation had planned for Baldy. For generations, Janss Investment had been turning ranchlands into commercial and residential developments in Southern California. The same sequence was played out in Brush Creek, as mountains, men and machines came together in a very sophisticated way. A team of young Janss executives was dispatched from Los Angeles to Brush Creek to gather data. Back in Los Angeles, the data were fed into a computer which, not surprisingly, suggested that hammers should come before nails and electric conduits before roads.

Fritz Benedict, who had owned land near Baldy for some time, had already explored the possibility of a ski area there with the Forest Service. He became principal architect for the Jansses. His assignment was simple: design a village that would serve the needs of skiers at a cost-profit ratio that the computer approved. As work proceeded on the nation's first computer-planned ski area, the pace of development accelerated all over the valley.

Snowmass-at-Aspen exemplified qualities that Aspen had itself eschewed—large scale, efficiency, group think and a no-nonsense cost-profit ratio. It was an anomaly in the landscape. In Brush Creek trees met sky unencumbered by the zigs and zags of modern houses. Old houses, barns and fences molded by eighty years of weather seemed part of the landscape. Defined by thick stands of trees, the meadows were fat with grass, and in the distance, layered mountains coldly marked the edge of the world. It was green, serene and sweet-smelling.

With its moat of swimming pools, Snowmass-at-Aspen ranged flat and gray and solid across the head of the valley. Functional, bleak, unconnected to the landscape, it looked not unlike a prison. At its center was a square with a clock tower and a fountain. Shops and restaurants ringed the square. Beyond them were lodges and condominiums; beyond them were the playing fields—ski slopes, golf course, tennis and paddle tennis courts. There were no roads in the village, and cars were corraled adjacent to it. The people who were attracted to Snowmass-at-Aspen drove nice, clean, expensive new cars; but in that planned pastoral setting cars would have intruded, reminding guests of America's endless freeways, pollution, traffic jams, sleazy fast-food parlors. In Snowmass-at-Aspen, everything was coordinated, modulated and adjusted to emulate either the good old days when the rich could escape the riffraff, or some future time when happy endings would be guaranteed. It promised endless fun, comfort, entertainment and surprises that were uniformly pleasant. It didn't want fidelity, allegiance or concern. It was not a town, but merely a kind of good-times machine, and the good times were organized and codified. They were also unreal.

The fact that there was a real town named Snowmass with a history, residents, houses and businesses just down the road was not seen by Janss people as a stumbling block. Market research indicated that Snowmass was a promising name for a ski resort and that the Aspen connection was worth millions in publicity. So, Janss built an instant town and named it after a celebrated real town and an obscure but happy village and compromised everyone in the process. The original Snowmass was ultimately forced to change its name to Old Snowmass. One resident said, "People that will take your name and use it don't care about anything."

Events proved him right. The Janss boys were not present to see their triumph. They sold out to American Cement and bought Sun Valley, the old Idaho ski resort where, Billy Janss said, "the power people, the excitement people are." Kingsbury Pitcher left Aspen too. He went first to southeastern New Mexico, where he designed Sierra Blanca, a new ski area owned by Robert O. Anderson, and later wound up buying the small Santa Fe Ski Basin from Anderson. It would never rival Aspen or Snowmass or even Sierra Blanca, would never be rich or famous. There was a kind of consolation in that for Pitcher. In Santa Fe he was finally out of the way of the high-stakes players, and safe.

The Janss boys and Pitcher were gone from the valley, but the mark they left behind was indelible. Bigger, cooler than anything that had gone before, Snowmass-at-Aspen worked on Aspen in fundamental ways.

A lot of people began moving into the new faster lane. Dunaway, the town's leading voice of reason, opened its first radio station, KSNO, in 1962 and put together a cable television company to bring Denver television to

Aspen via microwave. The fighting editor was on his way to becoming the valley's media king, and many people resented it because they resented his aggressive editorial policy. Conservatives remained leery of Dunaway. Shorty Pabst once told a magazine editor that Dunaway, with his "liberal" ideas, had done more damage to the valley than any other individual.

The puritan playboys, like the Janss boys, who came to Aspen in the 1960s were as restless as they were ambitious. They went about bagging places and projects in the way their fathers had bagged big game and their grandfathers had made the wilderness profitable. As it turned out, mountains could be merchandised in the same way that cars and detergents were merchandised. Ski pioneers were replaced by businessmen more interested in cost-profit ratios than high places, risk and adventure.

The Janss Investment Corporation attracted other speculators and developers; but it also brought young business and professional people. These young entrepreneurs saw Aspen as the ultimate suburb—interesting and beautiful, safe from the American commotion, a potential bonanza. Along with these ambitious burghers came more rebels, young people who had grown up in the suburbs of America and come to despise both the suburbs and America.

One of the best-selling books of the time was Eric Berne's *Games People Play*. The games were getting lethal. Lyndon Johnson exhorted his generals to "nail the coonskin to the wall" in Vietnam. Malcolm X, a black Muslim leader, was assassinated, and his followers blamed the government. Huge anti-war demonstrations were held around the country. In the Watts race riots in Los Angeles, thirty-five people were killed, 4,000 were arrested, and property damage reached $40 million. Ralph Nader went after the automotive industry in *Unsafe at Any Speed.* Op art, paintings that tricked the eye, was challenging pop art for the allegiance of the avant-garde. The Beatles became movie stars. Union wages had nearly doubled since 1949, and blue-collar workers were attacking anti-war protesters and longhairs in the streets. New York City suffered a blackout when a relay switch in Ontario failed, showing how complex and fragile our systems had become.

Both Russia and America put unmanned spacecraft on the moon. Dr. Michael E. De Bakey put artificial arteries in a thirty-seven-year-old woman. American students were reading *Quotations from Chairman Mao Tsetung.* Albert Schweitzer died.

Aspen's new young burghers bought existing businesses or opened new ones—stores, restaurants, real estate firms, insurance agencies, anything that they thought might succeed. Many were professionals—lawyers, dentists, architects, doctors. Some took up new occupations, others did the work they had always done. Most of them were married and had small children. They rented or bought houses, became active in organizations such as the Chamber of Commerce, the PTA and the Boosters Club, which promoted high school athletic teams. They skied, played tennis and picnicked in the high country.

Some new young rebels were so-called hippies, others were self-styled artists or writers, iconoclastic professionals, and people who rejected the very idea of careers and improvised their livings. A few were married, most were not. They rented apartments or cabins in the country, or built rough habitats in the wilderness. They were anti-organization, devotees of rock 'n' roll and various occult rites. Some of them skied.

From the start, the burghers and the rebels disliked and complained about each other. Each faction thought the other evil in some way. The burghers shared a common ground with the natives, the developers and speculators. They believed in growth and development, saw Aspen as a resort whose primary reason for being was profit. The young rebels were naturally allied with the more liberal older residents. They saw Aspen as a lovely small town and cherished its serenity, small scale and pastoral vistas. They didn't much like tourists, seeing them as a necessary evil. The rebels and liberals said, We're in Aspen for love, not money.

The long-simmering argument about the true meaning of Aspen that had begun years before between the natives and the newcomers grew noisier. The burghers had reason on their side: Aspen was a resort, wholly dependent on tourists. Without them the town would quickly wither. The rebels' response was passionate: the burghers, fatcats and speculators were turning the small town into Disneyland, selling the place rather than preserving it.

The burghers and their opponents were up-to-date versions of classic western figures. The mountain men had opposed the railroads, the settlers and anyone else who wanted to tame their turf. The miners hated the merchants who followed them into every town and sold the simplest goods for exorbitant prices. The cowboys hated the farmers who fenced them in. Now the rebels hated the burghers, and the Old West's favorite argument was brand-new.

The Old Westerners—the people who had been born

in the valley, the ranchers and cowboys—were allied with the merchants in this new battle. They had nothing against prosperity, they said, and in any case, they didn't like the long-haired eccentric rebels. But most of all, like their forebears, they didn't want anyone telling them what to do or how to do it.

10∧
Holding onto Camelot

J OHN KENNEDY's New Frontier had given way to Lyndon Johnson's Great Society, but in Aspen, Camelot
flourished. The Kennedys had begun coming regularly
to Aspen in 1962. The President never came, but everyone else did, including his wife, his children, his brothers
and most of the New Frontiersmen. The town's devotion
to sport and ideas made it a natural bivouac for them.
Bobby Kennedy participated in Institute seminars, skied
and climbed mountains in the area. Bob Craig became
his principal courtier in the mountains and dreamed
again of national prominence and power. As the Kennedys enjoyed Aspen, Aspen enjoyed them and left them
alone, as it always did with the famous and rich. An
Aspen resident would rather fall off a mountain than be
caught staring at a celebrity. But the Kennedys inevitably drew legions of photographers and reporters to
Aspen, and they were tireless, pursuing Kennedy children up the mountain, lurking in bushes outside the
Aspen Meadows, where the Kennedys usually stayed,
begging for quotes in restaurants.

The nation and the world were treated to an ava-
lanche of photos and stories about this Camelot in the
high country, shown all the glamour, speed and excite-

ment. Time had been tricked somehow in Aspen, stopped in its tracks. As the Great Society faltered, Aspen looked better and better to affluent America.

IN THE MID-SIXTIES, several new Institute trustees, chief among them New York art collectors John Powers and Armand Bartos, organized the Aspen Center for Contemporary Art. The first real addition to the Aspen cultural scene since Paepcke's death, it imported leading artists to Aspen for a summer of work and "happenings." The artists included Robert Indiana, Les Levine, Alan D'Arcangelo, Robert Morris, Claes Oldenburg, DeWain Valentine. Heavyweights, stars, come to Camelot.

One summer weekend the artists staged a happening in the Brand Building, a ramshackle Victorian building that had somehow been by-passed in the Great Restoration Period. Stan's Body Shop occupied the first floor of the building; the Center for Contemporary Art occupied the second floor. A sign on the entrance to the second floor stairs warned, "DO NOT ENTER. UNSAFE TO OCCUPY. Building Department, City of Aspen." But the artists had been granted a dispensation from the city for their happening.

Everyone was required to wear a black tie. Some people wore large brightly colored bow ties with BLACK printed on them. A few women tied thin black belts that looked like licorice whips truculently around their necks. Other women wore black dresses, which were judged by Bartos and Powers to be sufficient. They had a supply of black shoelaces to dispense to the tieless. A woman in a crunchy red stovepipe hat with a black tie on it said, "This is *fun.*"

The old staircase had been repainted by D'Arcangelo. Green grass, a highway vanishing over the horizon at the top of the stairs, blue sky, clouds. At the top of the stairs, a small room had been zapped up with cartoon lines of emphasis. There were black wiggly lines over the old cast-iron heater, hooks of lightning and KLIK over the light switch. A bass player, pianist and drummer were jamming coolly in the corner of the big north room that had previously housed recitals, ballet classes, archery tournaments and God knows what else. DeWain Valentine, smiling in a mocking way, was rocking gently to the music. His huge plastic structures, sketches and works in progress were set here and there around the room.

There was a bathroom with red lips on the walls. The walls of Les Levine's sanctum were padded with plastic modules, a few bright yellow, the rest white. "Independence Pass," a construction of undulating cylinders under varicolored changing lights, filled a small second room. Some children took their shoes off and vanished behind the "pass." They reappeared a few minutes later and said they liked it. The lights were like a sunset, moonlight, sunrise. Levine said the lights weren't representational, they were just lights.

Back in the hall, there was a line outside Claes Oldenburg's "chapel." It could accommodate only a few people at a time and was booked until after eight o'clock. His elegant drawings of a drum pedal hung on the wall. Various angles, various parts, all the same drum pedal.

In "the refreshment room," there were gangs of bananas, platoons of glasses of "altered water"—meaning water with green, yellow or red food dye in it. A sign stenciled on the floor of the next room said MORRIS. There were three arrangements of brown felt on the floor. Robert Morris was not present.

About ten large paintings hung on the walls of D'Arcangelo's studio. Roads. Highways. Some photographs of grain elevators and sketches were tacked up on one wall. D'Arcangelo stood in a corner, spent, exhausted-looking, watching the people looking at his work.

It was fun, perhaps even edifying, but it was not pre- posterous, and that was the one thing it was meant to be. Camelot had got very orderly. When kings die, there is a terrible need in the people for order.

MASSIVE AND UNDISTINGUISHED condominiums were rising in midtown Aspen. New residential neighbor- hoods, suburbs, were being developed on the perimeter of the town. Some tried to combine houses and the land- scape in congenial ways, but others followed standard suburban formulas, revealing the same sense of life at work that one saw in countless American suburbs—big new cars, passionately tended lawns, the lust for things.

"The Master Plan" was inspired by the condominiums and new suburbs. It was initiated by Bayer, Benedict and Glidden; prepared by the Leo A. Daley Company of San Francisco; paid for under terms of the 1954 Housing Act with funds from the Housing and Home Financing Agency, the city and county and the Aspen Institute; approved by city and county officials in 1966; and ap- plauded by both burghers and rebels. It was to be our salvation.

When it was approved, 2,300 people lived in Aspen and its immediate environs, with accommodations for about 6,000 visitors. About 1,000 people resided in the rest of the county. Though the plan was technically called the Aspen Area General Plan, it was, from the first, familiarly known as the Master Plan.

It defined itself as "a broad long-term policy statement on the goals of the city and county to which specific decisions necessary to the daily conduct of affairs must be related if urban-growth forecast for the next twenty years is to assume a desired pattern and direction . . . the General Plan does not directly regulate the use of private land; but zoning legislation, which does regulate the use of private land, must be in conformity with and in furtherance of the General Plan."

It said that "the distinction between urban and rural uses has been blurred as development has spread onto Red and Smuggler Mountains and along Castle and Maroon Creeks." It was the purpose of the plan "to retain the fine balance between man and his environment, the essence of Aspen's character.

"The planning area is envisioned as a unique human settlement, culturally and recreationally oriented, with an urban pattern characterized by a dispersed system of commercial and accommodation centers, each immediately surrounded by relatively densely settled residential neighborhoods. The further reaches between the centers are envisioned as being in urban use, but at a density and scale to create a feeling of separation between and emphasize the distinction of centers. An overlying pattern of cultural and educational facilities, unified through creation of open spaces, parkways and trails ensures the livability of the community as does the circulation system, connecting all places of commercial, industrial and other social activity. Enhanced by a setting of scenic mountainous terrain, the community will offer outstanding contrast to other contemporary urban settings. . . ."

The Master Plan specifically recommended that the north side of the valley remain predominantly rural and residential; the rest of the valley remain farms and forests; and population densities in nearly every area of the county be dramatically reduced. Because traffic was thought to be a serious problem, the plan also recommended a light-rail transit system between Aspen and Snowmass, as well as a transportation center, city buses and parking structures. In addition, it suggested the creation of a system of parks, playgrounds and trails and the construction of a civic center.

Pitkin County measures 950 square miles, or three-quarters the size of the state of Rhode Island. In 1966 it had less than 10,000 beds. By 1985, according to the plan, the number of beds would triple. You could probably lose 30,000 people in a mountainous county measuring almost 1,000 square miles and not find them for several days. By American standards, this problem of ours was a joke. But by our standards, ruin was on the way. The Master Plan became our Bible, our Declaration of Independence. The rebels liked it because it ensured controlled growth. The burghers liked it because it ensured orderly growth—the sort that affluent America would approve of, the sort that would keep the rabble out and keep prices up. Aspen would become a seller's market, and the burghers would be the primary sellers.

With the Master Plan in hand, the dour weight of history and the thousand precedents notwithstanding, Aspen believed it could outwit destiny. It could be rich and famous and beautiful and true all at once. It could combine a vigorous and expanding economy with lovely and serene prospects. It could have everything.

STILL, MAYOR "SHORTY" PABST deplored what he saw as evidence of moral decline. Claiming that Aspen schoolchildren were trafficking in drugs, he pushed for a grand jury investigation of immorality and illegalities in Aspen. District Attorney John Wendt, who doubled as Master of the Aspen Valley Hunt (which chased coyotes or scented rags due to the absence of fox in the mountains), was happy to oblige the mayor.

The grand jury turned up no concrete evidence of crime and issued no indictments. There were rumors, never substantiated, of phone taps, illegal searches, informal surveillance. A sixteen-year-old girl was subpoenaed to testify and later claimed she was not informed of her rights in the proceedings, and was harassed during her testimony. Bitter and sick at their daughter's treatment by the grand jury and what they felt to be unwarranted invasions of their own privacy, her parents sold their house and left Aspen with all of their children. They were leading citizens, people of substance, and in this citadel of freedom and civility, they believed that their teen-aged daughter had been treated like a hardened criminal.

Bugsy Barnard challenged Pabst for the mayoralty in 1965. After a dire struggle, Barnard won. Unwilling to leave the arena, Pabst founded a second newspaper, the *Aspen Illustrated News,* with some other Skiing Corporation directors. When the other directors tired of the expensive and unprofitable vehicle, Pabst became sole owner, publisher and editor. He railed against Barnard, Dunaway, the presence of so-called hippies in Aspen and the continuing moral decline of the place.

For two tumultuous terms, Barnard was synonymous with politics in Aspen. He wasted little time in soliciting the opinions of other people, expected absolute loyalty from his friends and allies, and was unforgiving of those he thought had let him down. He was a seat-of-the-pants pol, an improviser. Like Pabst, he pushed for a steady escalation of city services and budgets, yet took occasional and dramatic stands against developers. When plans for the town's largest condominium to date, Aspen

Square, were made public, Barnard declared an emergency and imposed an immediate moratorium on building in Aspen. The sewer plant, he said, was overloaded. This may have been so, but his maneuver was judged just that in court, and work on the condominium proceeded. Bil Dunaway and Barnard divided on the Aspen Square question. When Barnard subsequently tried to drive his own city attorney out of office, Dunaway scolded Mayor Barnard again editorially. Barnard responded by accusing Dunaway of being a traitor to the cause.

But the "cause" was increasingly unclear. Barnard seemed simultaneously to want to build a city and to preserve Aspen's small scale. His views on civil liberties were equally contradictory. When Pabst attacked the "hippies," Barnard defended them. But during his administration, civil liberties took as bad a beating as they had during Pabst's era.

Claiming that the longhairs were driving away legitimate tourists and "tarnishing Aspen's image," Aspen's burghers presented a petition to the council, asking for a "crackdown" on the longhairs. A councilman concurred, saying, "There are lots of people who wear beards. I'm talking about the ones who are leeches and walk around dirty with their little sunflowers on their bibs. . . . The community is right now ready to have some people harassed. Policemen began rounding up longhairs on vagrancy charges and bringing them into City Magistrate Guide Meyer's court. Typically, the Swiss restaurateur, a long-time critic of "hippies," gave one youth ninety days in jail and a $300 fine for "blocking the sidewalk." The young man said plaintively, "If I'd known I was blocking the sidewalk, I would have moved."

The Pitkin County Bar Association protested Meyer's tactics. Two hundred and fifty people attended a reorganization meeting of the Aspen chapter of the American Civil Liberties Union. Pabst's *Aspen Illustrated News* gave full editorial support to Meyer and the cops. Dunaway criticized them in the *Times*. Virtually everyone took sides.

Joe Edwards, a young lawyer recently arrived from Texas, filed suit in federal court in Denver against the city on behalf of the longhairs. The judge issued a warning to the city: "The Police Department of the City of Aspen, from the chief through the assistant, on down to the patrolmen, has acted with undue aggressiveness toward this class of persons." About Meyer, he said, "It is a blot on the judicial system that this lasted as long as it did." The federal judge concluded that if the situation did not improve, he would take action against the city. Meyer was fired. The city's unconstitutional vagrancy ordinance was repealed, but the divisions remained.

Later, when five dynamite blasts rocked the town on the Fourth of July, the police imposed a curfew. The sheriff called for a posse from Glenwood Springs to reinforce his own squad. Meyer claimed it was the work of Communists; and Barnard blamed the whole sequence on "hippie-haters." The subsequent investigation was inconclusive. It located neither the people who set off the blasts nor the reasons for them.

Like Pabst, Bugsy Barnard behaved in increasingly imperial ways, and appeared to see himself alone on the barricades. By the end of his second term, the exemplary liberal had become the leading conservative spokesman. The search for a new Big Daddy had gone badly in the sixties. The men we chose to lead us—Pabst and Barnard —were as different as men could be when they took office, and as similar as men could be when they left.

Ironically, the only American issue to reach Aspen in

the 1960s was civil liberties—the one issue we thought we had resolved years before. It was a bitter moment in Aspen, which suddenly looked more like Dodge City than Camelot, and it was a turning point. The place split wide open. A kind of anarchy surfaced. The freewheeling town had become a free-for-all. Fundamental questions had been raised and left unanswered. Nothing was guiding Aspen now but its own momentum.

ON THE EVENING OF JUNE 5, 1968 Hunter Thompson, Billy Noonan and I sat in my bedroom and watched ABC's coverage of the California primary. Robert F. Kennedy was running against Senator Eugene McCarthy for the Democratic Presidential nomination. A victory in California was crucial to Kennedy. We wanted him to win it all—the primary, the nomination and the Presidency. Like us, Kennedy was a rebel, and we believed the only man who could save the country from predators like Johnson and Nixon. We not only admired him, we loved him. He was the only hero left in the arena. His brother had been gunned down five years before; Martin Luther King, two months before.

Noonan had drifted into Aspen several years before to see Semonin and Thompson, his old Kentucky friends. He'd stayed, working at a variety of jobs, "a ski bum who doesn't ski," someone said. Thompson had gone to San Francisco in 1965 and written a book about the Hell's Angels, the notorious California motorcycle gang. In a rush of chemical logic, the Angels concluded that Thompson was getting rich writing about them and therefore they would beat him to death. Only the intervention of a very large Angel named Tiny saved him. He came back to Aspen immediately after the beating, his nose broken, his ribs cracked, his rage enormous.

Bobby Kennedy won the primary, made a short passionate speech, and left the ballroom of the Ambassador Hotel in Los Angeles. Thompson, Noonan and I cheered and clapped and drank to Kennedy and ourselves. It would be all right now. ABC cut back to Joey Bishop's talk show. Thompson and Noonan left. I went into my kitchen to wash the glasses and ashtrays. There was shouting, screaming from the television set. ABC had cut back to the Ambassador. Bobby Kennedy had been shot in the hotel kitchen. I began to curse, cry. Thompson and Noonan heard it on their car radio and returned. We drank and smoked through the night, watching, waiting. Kennedy wasn't dead. No one seemed to know how badly he was hurt. Noonan said several times, "I have the feeling I should call someone, but I don't know who." At dawn Thompson and Noonan left. As he was getting into his car, Thompson said, "It won't be like the last time." I believed him. I had to. I decided that if I didn't sleep, Kennedy wouldn't die. I repeated Thompson's words over and over again to myself, to other people. He did die, of course. We were like vagrants in the world.

One Saturday Semonin and I set off down Highway 82, going nowhere, just going. Cars from all over America cafoomed by us while horses stood still in pastures. People rushing, horses standing still. In small matters, life is eventually just. Little golf carts that looked like beetles on speed scooted along the golf course fairways. Thirty-five or forty sleek small planes were parked at the airport. Billows of dust rolled up out of the Gerbazdale gravel pit. The Gerbazdale Trailer Court looked like an

unfinished movie set. The site of the Lazy Glen Trailer
Court ten miles down the road, with its utility connec-
tions rising out of the ground at military intervals, resembled an empty drive-in movie theater.

We passed Basalt's big new shopping center, saw a few
fishermen standing poised and easy in the river, more
gravel pits, more new houses, pastel and clumsy like high
school girls, clinging to the road. Bob's TV-and-Every-
thing displayed a television set with an unboxed picture
tube, a great flat glazed eye, one of Dr. T. J. Eckleburg's
eyes rolled inevitably west, chasing the green light.

We went back to the shopping center. In the grocery
store, there were jars of mustard and mayonnaise as
large as lamp bases, cheeses with cinderblock proportions. A sign admonished, "Keep America Beautiful with
Lady Finger Garden Gloves." John Updike's *Assorted
Prose* sat in a rack next to the checkout counter. There
were mountains of notebooks, trees of ballpoint pens.
We didn't buy anything. Overcooked air was bouncing
off the asphalt in the parking lot. We drove back to
Aspen.

It was cool and quiet. Its tree-lined streets were
empty. Sprinklers blurred the air, making small rainbows. It was lovely, but it was not Camelot. There was
no Camelot. America, with its gravel pits and giant
cheeses and planes and pastel houses, was closing in.

Che Guevera died. So did Alice B. Toklas, Langston
Hughes, J. Robert Oppenheimer, Dorothy Parker, Tal-
lulah Bankhead and Woody Guthrie. Mickey Mouse celebrated his fortieth birthday. Jacqueline Kennedy married Aristotle Onassis. The Vietnam War got wider and
bigger. So did the demonstrations against it. During the
1968 Democratic National Convention in Chicago,
American cops and soldiers beat and gassed American

citizens. Thompson was in Chicago and was clubbed by a cop, gassed and shoved through a store window. He sent me his press badge on which he had scrawled, "This entitles bearer to a beating." Several months later Richard M. Nixon moved into the White House.

11 ⌃
Things Aloft
in the Evening

THERE IS NO middle ground in the Roaring Fork Valley. In the midst of a blizzard, it is impossible to imagine the end of it. And when the sun shines on windless days, one cannot imagine improvements or endings. Temperatures rise or fall forty degrees in an hour. High winds rake the valley and make it jumpier than New York at midnight, but usually there is no wind at all.

The beauty of the place is endless, but it never repeats. After a snowstorm everything is diamonds and whipped cream, blissful curves, immaculate. In all seasons the mountains rise higher than one can see and are deeper than one can know. There is no place where one can stand and see it whole. From a plane one sees only enormous and baffling wrinkles and tucks. The geologists can tell us how it came to be that way but not why.

SPRING IN THE VALLEY is devious. It tempts you to dream of soft sweet days and flowers breaking through the stiff ground and clouds of green overtaking the starchy skeletons of cottonwoods and aspen, and then it boils and storms. Spring snow is deceitful. It is only a distant relation of winter snow. It doesn't crunch under your boots, but slurps. Footprints are brown. The sky vanishes for days at a time, taking the sun with it, leaving behind a dirty gray vault. People become cranky. Winter has a time and place, and both have passed, but it still has you in its grip. The calendar is a liar. Tempers decorate the unfavorable air in shades of blue. Children are restless. Twenty minutes ago, the other day, last week they wheeled their bikes through strings of sparkling puddles. Now they are shoveling snow again. Skiing is a tricky enterprise, full of rocks and soft places. Snowballs have muddy hearts.

The clouds crack suddenly. The sun comes out and the snow disappears from everywhere but the north side of things. The greening proceeds cautiously. Summer dreams are irresistible. The air is soft and warm. But winter has not gone away. It is simply lurking behind the mountains, gathering its waning strength for another assault. It is crippled, blind in one eye, but still capable of making trouble. Hints of green drown in the spreading white. Clouds settle on rooftops. There are no mountains. The world is only 200 feet wide again.

This cycle of resurrection and revocation repeats itself over and over again. The birds are back and during snowstorms they sing. The birds know that there will be a happy ending and they do not have calendars and clocks, so they are not impatient.

THE SUMMER DAY begins in absolute silence. The sky is black, then inky blue, then pale. The sun touches the top of Bell Mountain, spilling down the slopes. The sun itself is not yet visible. It lingers lazily behind Smuggler Mountain. Just before it appears, its flaming rim seers through a fringe of trees on Smuggler's spine.

The air is cool and green at dawn, but turns warm and golden by noon. It's full of summer: the smell of cut grass, the smell of the river, wet and high and fast, the smell of flowers, the smell of heat. Sometimes, one can smell the sea though it's 1,200 miles west and 8,000 feet down. Or perhaps it's just the airs of boundlessness.

The joggers, the easy riders, the children come out. The joggers look tense, somber, as if to impress the more indolent with their nobility. Their arms end in fists. The easy riders are more pleasant to see. They fly by leaning back on their seats, their arms crossed in satisfaction. Ten-speed bikes come in wonderful colors, always look new.

Summer light is profound, true. It is perfect for painters with Mediterranean inclinations, poets full of juices, physicists who dream of quarks, strangeness and charm, musicians who imagine notes that have not yet been reached.

The children are drunk. They invent games. They walk backward down the street very fast. They sit down, stand up, laugh. Everyone wins. They perform complicated jobs. They cut a few blades of grass with scissors. They stack wood and unstack it. They try to set lawns on fire with magnifying glasses. They suck ants through straws.

In the West End, two white mules and a white pony sing to each other. In the late afternoon, cars thud by the mules on their way to the tent. Many people walk to the tent. They dress casually. Levi's predominate. Musicians in white coats and black ties walk to work. People sing to themselves. A few conduct.

Heat has been piling up in the tent all day. There are ladies in garden-party dresses, men in ties. There are long slim young people in bare feet and scraps of denim and tee shirts. There are men in leisure suits with wide shirt collars lying flat on their collarbones. There are women in tidy traveling outfits. There are intellectuals in beards and clumsy clothes that demonstrate their disdain for fashion. Their smiles are superior.

Finally everyone has found the perfect place to sit. Some sit upright inside. Others sprawl flat on the grass outside. The music begins. Gentle coaxing, artful fingers, sturdy souls are required to loosen the sounds hidden in catgut and old wood. The audience is reverent. A universe of sound and light and air is made under that reaching canvas. When it is done, everyone is used up, a little lost, subdued.

Sometimes on late summer afternoons, heavy dark clouds boil up in the western sky and charge up the valley. Scudding, hard sheets of rain blister windows, make small rivers in the street, clean and polish everything. Afterward the sky's surface is complex—streaks of light, trailing scarves of clouds—and you can smell oceans in the dusky air. Time and fish and almost everything are aloft in the evening.

People go to the mall to sit at tables and drink wine, walk about, look at each other. Music students play Bach and Mozart on street corners for pennies. Glitter kids come out to play. They move to some odd beat, challenging everyone with their eyes. Their hair is perfectly cut.

In dark bars, people shout, drink, make bets on anything. Carpenters still plaster-dusted stand next to ladies in silk dresses from Lake Forest.

Enormous feasts are prepared in fifty kitchens. The smell of food mingles with the smell of beer and suntan oil and marijuana in the streets. Glasses hit glasses, a thousand toasts are drunk.

In bookstores, people look hopefully for the one book that will explain everything, sit defiantly in corners and read.

People fight sometimes, for reasons that are not clear. Other people dance. Lewd acts are occasionally performed.

The neighborhoods are silent again. Empty rectangles of light mark the houses. Everything goes on in those houses.

FALL ARRIVES SHY, but grows quickly confident. It seizes the mountain with colors so dense they cannot be named. The fall light is exact, generous, pure. In that light it is impossible to picture disappointment, defeat, deformity. The fall sky is as soft as an old workshirt. It is high, handsome and constant.

Everything is in motion, preparing to lie quiet and easy under the snow, reducing itself to essentials, a fine brown skeleton of itself, shadows and light alloyed, almost gone.

On the crystal days of fall, the streets are still, the meadows pliant, dogs loopy, magpies—those alley fighters of birds—efficient. Ducks are busy in Hallam Lake, landing, leaving, skating across the water trailing nets of ripples. People stand still, talk very slowly of nothing, watch the eloquent sky, thoughtfully pop fallen leaves under their boots. People are overtaken by antic postures, anarchic acts, old jokes. Fall keeps all of its promises, if there's time.

The nights are cold, envoys sent ahead by winter, but Afternoons are warm. On fall mornings small isolate pools of light spread down and down from the highest mountain reaches and fill the whole valley. The day does with light what Mozart did with sound.

In the fall one can suddenly remember all the falls. The first is as clear as, or clearer than, all the others. The years gone by are as coherent as a string of pearls. It all makes sense. For a moment one can see that one thing did indeed lead to the other. But the moment passes. Absolute logic can only be borne for a moment. One can look ahead, down the long unnamed years and see all the unannotated thrills and terrors lining the way. The other seasons do not give that perspective, that sense of time unfolding forever. Summer and winter are boundaried times. Spring is a pause, a lapse, a portion.

Fall is perishable. It goes in a blink or it hangs on, bruised, limp, cut. One hopes for one obliterating snowstorm, a great blast of snow and arctic air, or for the sun stalled forever on fall's lucid axis.

THERE IS NO NAME for the season of pale skies and confused airs that comes after fall and before winter. Fall's signs are gone, but the clever wizards of winter haven't arrived yet. It's the interim.

Snow comes in the night and vanishes as one looks at it. It's windy, gray, so sparse and dim as to be a kind of night. The color has run out of the landscape and the sky. Even the shadows lack style. Sometimes in the early morning there is a certain brightness, but by noon it has shattered on itself, broken, and rolled wanly down.

Under gunmetal skies, life proceeds oddly. The birds are ugly. Halloween and Thanksgiving, witches and pilgrims come together in the mind. It's hollow, the interim. Laughter is tinny, manic. Furnaces rev up and rattle back to work. Cars gag on morning frost. The valley is tubercular. We need the interim in the way the boxer needs his sparring partner.

WINTER IS THE DAZZLING SEASON. Everything pales next to the crystal landscape that emerges out of the winter dawn.

One day the snow begins and it deepens steadily, inexorably, and the perimeters of the valley close and close. It becomes a stunning monument to cold. Sometimes it snows in such a very dense and serious way you think it's never going to stop. All the sharp edges vanish. Fences become long drapes. Some things vanish entirely. Brightly painted Victorian houses loom like great gray ghosts. The squeaks and grinds of life are muffled. Cars move through the streets as slowly and quietly as sailboats. People become vague drifting shadows. Trees and bushes become pale sculptures. Dogs are confused.

Perspective is distorted. The world seems very close, intimate, but things in the world seem remote. Buildings are small, very far away, lacking substance. The eye is constantly tricked. The mountains are gone. You know they're there, you can feel them looming, but you can't see them. It's not a cause for alarm. Disappearance is not departure.

The snow falls and falls and then it stops falling. It's oblivious to our feelings in the matter. It comes when the right elements mingle in the right proportions and it stops when those elements separate. It multiplies, and subdues us, and that is not a bad thing from time to time.

In such a climate one becomes a creature of extremes, wanting no snow or a lot of it rising like a slow, slow flood, spreading out in wide, unbroken plains. Snow so deep that one must move through as if it were the ocean. This climate spoils one for more decorous latitudes. One wants not merely weather, but swashbuckling, high-stepping, prancing weather. One savors extremes in events and people, prefers drama to dailiness.

OUR DESTINIES, Aspen's and mine, had become inextricably entwined. It was not just that I had spent sixteen years there. Many people spend their entire lives in dark and alien places for reasons of necessity, lassitude, money, family, misapprehended duty, misplaced loyalty, and they remain unconnected. But the same rhythm moved in us, the place and me. We seemed to rise and fall to the same beat, to shudder and shout simultaneously, to mourn and dream in the same proportions. We fell for the same tricks, scams, delusions, and recovered with the same appetite for more. These things happen.

I had tried to resist, to turn my back, to skip out on the beat. I had even tried to leave. But I always came back to that odd and encouraging landscape, that weird and thrilling weather. It was often uncomfortable, that union, and based more in passion than in sense.

In the 1960s Aspen had gone from one extreme to the other, from pastoral town to boom town. It had been Camelot and Dodge City. The eccentrics' hideout was becoming affluent America's playground. We hated and feared America, but America was still in love with us, for we were everything it was not. It came to Aspen in the way that cripples go to Lourdes.

Judy Garland and Jack Kerouac died. Senator Edward Kennedy drove into a pond at Chappaquiddick, and Mary Jo Kopechne was killed. Charlie Manson and his followers were tried for killing Sharon Tate and four other people. The Chicago Eight went on trial for fomenting a riot. One hundred people were killed in California mud slides. Food additives were linked to cancer. Lieutenant William Calley was tried for massacring Vietnamese civilians at My Lai. President Nixon appointed Warren Burger as Chief Justice of the U.S. Supreme Court. Three hundred thousand people went to Woodstock to hear rock 'n' roll. Hundreds of thousands of others demonstrated around the country against the war. Neil Armstrong walked on the moon. In the first rock musical, *Hair,* they sang of the dawning of the Age of Aquarius. Dennis Hopper summed it all up in *Easy Rider* when he said, "We blew it."

In Aspen we thought America was gone, we were all that was left of it. A growing number of us thought that we knew better than Brown, Pabst, Barnard and all the others. We set out to take control.

12▴
The Aspen Technique

ASPEN DID NOT bother with city elections from 1917 to 1927. From 1927 to 1962 elections were polite rituals. In the early sixties Pabst and Barnard made politics in the valley combative, controversial and vital. In 1969 New Politics turned up in Aspen.

New Politics, a phenomenon of the 1960s, was actually old politics, dating back to the first decades of the country when the people, not the bosses, were in charge. In the 1960s, the Reverend Martin Luther King found support not among the nation's leaders but among its citizens, white as well as black. Senator Eugene McCarthy had enrolled thousands of young and essentially apolitical workers. Bobby Kennedy had spoken passionately of participatory democracy and seen the outsiders—the blacks, the poor, the young, the blue-collar workers—as his natural constituents. It was a promising effort at takeup politics away from the politicians and returning it to the people. But King and Kennedy were killed, and Nixon, the quintessential politician, took the White House. By 1969 New Politics was floundering nationally but thriving in Aspen. America may be lost, we said, but Aspen will be saved by the people.

An amalgam of long-time liberal residents and new

young rebels formed a lobbying group, Citizens for
Community Action. CCA organized neighborhood cau-
cuses that met regularly to identify problems and discuss
priorities. Its leaders included Joe Edwards, "the hippie
lawyer," and his colleague Dwight Shellman. Its first test
was the 1969 city election.

Barnard chose not to run for a third term and picked
Leonard Oates, a quiet young lawyer, as his successor.
They were temperamental opposites, but politically
compatible. Conservative Oates favored low taxes and
efficient city management—meaning little or no public
interference in private enterprise. Eve Homeyer, a mid-
dle-age businesswoman who had been a leader of the
anti-longhair movement and a functionary in the state
Republican party, announced her candidacy too.

The CCA had found some candidates for the city council, but had no one to run for mayor. Neither Hunter
Thompson nor I were members of the group, but we
were in general agreement with their direction and
goals, and on hearing of Mrs. Homeyer's candidacy, we
decided to act. An Oates-Homeyer contest was no contest, we said, and we made a list of possible alternative
candidates. Although neither of us had met Joe Edwards,
we kept coming back to his name. He was young, a
fighter who had battled to preserve civil liberties in
Aspen and had already spoken out against runaway
growth. After talking with novelist James Salter, a CCA
activist, we called Edwards. It was midnight, we were
strangers, and he was suspicious at first, then ambivalent,
but he finally agreed to run. Our crusade to save Aspen
was underway.

As Edwards was a political novice, Thompson became
the chief theoretician for our side. He'd lived in San
Francisco during the period when Haight-Ashbury

changed from a good-natured freewheeling neighborhood into a sleazy venal circus. He had been beaten by
both outlaws and cops. As a journalist, he had become a
leading critic of what he saw clearly to be national madness and of its maker, Richard Nixon. Now he set about
to galvanize the outsiders in Aspen and to topple the
insiders. If it worked here, he said, it could work anywhere. He wrote screeds on every issue. I had become
the principal columnist for the *Aspen Times,* and my
newspaper ads for Edwards echoed my "Talk of the
Times" columns. Posing such questions as "When Will
Aspen Become the Place You Left?" and "Aspen—
1984?," the ads used photographs of acres of tract houses
and surreal freeway cloverleafs. Each concluded with
the same line: "There is still time. Vote for Joe Edwards
for mayor." Thompson and I saw the CCA as a vehicle
for New Politics and we saw ourselves as anti-politicians,
but our ad campaign was sophisticated in the best political tradition. Some people, in fact, said it was slick.

A platform, style and vocabulary emerged early.
"Greedheads" and "land rapers" were villified in radio
ads. Flutist Herbie Mann's mournful recording of "The
Battle Hymn of the Republic" was our campaign theme
song. Tom Benton, who had left a promising architectural practice in Los Angeles to become an Aspen artist,
designed silk-screen posters that artfully exhorted residents to "save" Aspen. Newspaper ads featured growing
lists of Edwards supporters, who ranged from some of
Aspen's more solid citizens to the somewhat raffish heirs
to great American fortunes to self-described "freaks"
and "dopers." A large group of volunteers, most of whom
had no previous political experience, worked to register
voters, solicit public statements of support for Edwards,
raise money, publicize the issues and get supporters'

names for the ads. At one point, overcome by our own cleverness and importance, Thompson and I told the volunteer responsible for assembling the lists of supporters that familiar names were preferable to nobodies. She got very angry and said she thought the Edwards campaign was about "nobodies." We backed down quickly and ruefully.

That night Thompson said that politics was addictive, and we must watch ourselves very carefully for signs of addiction. But if Barnard and Pabst had made politics central in Aspen, we proceeded to make it everything. Prompted by Thompson and me, Edwards spoke of Aspen in the way that Populists had spoken of America a century before, portraying the developers and speculators as villains who would destroy the valley for their own profit. We called for stringent measures to preserve the beauty and character of the place.

In a long article in *Rolling Stone* magazine in October 1970, Thompson reviewed our anti-politics movement. He wrote that we wanted to "create a town where people could live like human beings, instead of slaves to some bogus sense of Progress that is driving us all mad."

He also defined our strategy. "This is the essence of what some people call 'the Aspen technique' in politics: neither opting out of the system nor working within it, but calling its bluff by using its strength to turn it back on itself . . . and by always assuming the people in power were not smart." By the end of the Edwards campaign, I was convinced, despite my lifelong bias to the contrary, that the law was actually on our side. Not the cops or the judges or the politicians—the actual law itself as printed in the dull and musty lawbooks that we constantly had to consult because we had no other choice. . . .

Journalism requires a skeptical mind, a certain distance. Thompson and I had become zealots, overnight believers. We believed in ourselves, our candidate and our vision of Aspen. We suffered no doubts about the wisdom of our cause, put no tough questions to ourselves. As the campaign wound down, a friend remarked, "You have real power, you know." Because journalists are supposed to eschew power, publically at least, I asked modestly, "What do you mean?" My friend replied, "I asked Fritz Benedict why he was supporting Joe Edwards and he said because you told him to." I wish I could say that I was horrified at the idea that I had enlisted one of the town's leading citizens on our side so easily. I wasn't. I was pleased. Whether or not I actually had power, I loved the idea of having it and using it. It was my turn, I thought, to have my way with Aspen. The Edwards campaign was for me a life-or-death struggle.

Thin, trim, conservatively dressed, Leonard Oates went through the ritual listlessly, apparently willing to leave the outcome to fate and Bugsy Barnard. Eve Homeyer, with her pale red hair, the wardrobe of a country club matron and a sharp tongue, was our true adversary. She stressed the need for moderation and fiscal conservatism. She spoke of Oates and Edwards in the way a pro speaks of amateurs. She was quite willing to support anything that might win votes for her, and frequently noted that while she was a traditionalist who understood and appreciated the free enterprise system, she was also an innovator who would seek ways to control anyone who wanted to take advantage of the system. Her principal asset, however, was that she was not anything like Edwards. Edwards scared a great many people, was called "a socialist" and worse. Many men who had theretofore believed that a woman's place was in the kitchen or the bedroom rallied around Mrs. Homeyer because she was the only thing standing between them and an Edwards victory.

As election day approached, the town was overcome by a kind of frenzy. Edwards was the subject of anonymous mailings and vague unsubstantiated charges of wrongdoing. In an odd turnabout, the once conservative *Aspen Illustrated News,* now owned and run by former mayor Pabst's son Nicholas, backed Edwards, and Bil Dunaway backed Mrs. Homeyer.

Dunaway was away from Aspen when the editorial appeared, but came back to vote. When he went to his polling place on election morning, he was accosted by Tom Benton and other Edwards supporters. They accused him of backing Mrs. Homeyer from the beginning but leaving town when the actual endorsement ran so as not to taint his liberal reputation. Dunaway replied that since he was planning to be away, he had left the endorsement to his staff. Associate editor George Madsen had overridden the staff and endorsed Mrs. Homeyer on his own. Edwards teams were deployed at all of the polling places because we thought the old pols might try to intimidate new young voters, but Benton's verbal assault on Dunaway was the most heated moment of the day. This was a great disappointment to us because we had been prepared to tape all instances of intimidation and expose the bullies once and for all.

When the ballots were counted, Mrs. Homeyer had won by a 6-vote margin. Some of Edwards's supporters claimed that the absentee ballots had been mailed out too late for voters to get tham back to Aspen by election day. Some concrete evidence did exist to support the theory, so we made phone calls to places as remote as Guatemala and the Himalayas to substantiate it. We turned up several people who said they had voted for

Edwards and whose ballots were late getting back to Aspen, but not enough of them. We abandoned the effort, but resolved to stay in the arena.

Though Mrs. Homeyer had won the election, a fundamental shift had occurred. The new city council was younger and more liberal than any previous council. Its most liberal member was Ned Vare, a pacific anti-pol who had rejected an offer of expertise and aid from Thompson and me, campaigned quietly, and won by a large margin. He proved to be shrewd and capable. With the support of three other liberal councilmen, Vare managed to turn city hall in a new direction. Though we suffered one defeat, we were on our way to capturing the castle, driving out all the would-be Big Daddies, and making Aspen an absolute democracy.

CCA and PARK, another liberal lobbying group that specialized in park and open-space acquisitions, pushed the city council for everything that Edwards had promised in his campaign platform, including municipal purchase of open space, an increase in the sales tax to raise funds for conservation measures, a full-time city-county planner, tighter zoning, density and growth controls. One by one these things were accomplished during Mrs. Homeyer's mayoralty.

13 ^
Writs of Assumption

THE SEVENTIES BEGAN BADLY. Four hundred and forty-eight American colleges and universities were closed down by student strikes. The President called the students "bums." The National Guard shot and killed four student bystanders during an anti-war demonstration at Kent State University in Ohio. The economy slumped. Gold dropped below the official price of $35 an ounce, and the Dow-Jones average sagged to 631, lower than it had been since 1962. But in Aspen, the boom was accelerating at a dangerous rate. Money was being made by many, fortunes by a few. Aspen was no longer a small town and not yet a city, but it was too contrary to be a resort. Novelist Saul Bellow, who spent several summers in Aspen, feared it might become "a pleasure slum."

Between 1950 and 1960 Pitkin County's population increased 44.7 percent. Between 1960 and 1970 it rose 158.9 percent. In 1950, 639 people held jobs in the county; in 1960 there were 1,040; in 1970, 2,847. In 1950, more than a quarter of the county's workers were engaged in agriculture. By 1970 only 4 percent were still on the land. In 1950 only 87 people were in trade. By 1970, 646 were in trade, and more significantly, there were 1,036 in services such as lodging, banking, ski instructing. Though the population was growing and the number of jobs was increasing rapidly, one survey showed that family income declined appreciably as tourism became the county's dominant industry.

Workers expressed their discontent in frightening ways: a wave of arson, dynamite blasts on Aspen Mountain and at an ersatz windmill at the new subdivision of Holland Hills, bomb threats at a school and bank. The Aspen Ski Patrol joined the Teamsters and went out on strike, but received little sympathy from either resident or visiting skiers. They cut the Teamster tie and went back to work.

Businessmen reorganized the Aspen Chamber of Commerce and Visitors Bureau into a larger and more aggressive promotional organization. Business had never been better, and the operative word was MORE. At the same time city officials, alarmed by the growing boom, set up a Goals Task Force to prepare a long-range agenda of priorities.

Aspen Skiing Corporation president D. R. C. Brown wrote an open letter to the city in which he said: "It seems a reasonable assumption that in less than ten years, the Aspen area will have a guest capacity of at least twice the capacity of its ski slopes. If this is permitted to happen, the inevitable result will be crowded slopes, long lift lines and poor skiing conditions. What this will do to Aspen's reputation as one of the world's finest ski resorts, we leave to your imagination.

"Property owners or developers planning additional developments in lodges, condominiums, etc., should be aware that the Aspen Skiing Corporation feels a responsibility to both the public and its stockholders to provide its customers with the best and safest skiing conditions possible. The day may come when, in order to accomplish this, we will have to place some limit on the number of skiers we permit to use our facilities in any one day.

"The purpose of this letter is to call your attention to a problem while there is still time to seek a solution to it. It is our hope that a public awareness of the direction in which we are heading may avert an economic disaster for Pitkin County."

Brown's letter pleased liberals and upset businessmen, but it only confused residents. It wasn't clear whether he was calling for a general cooling of the boom or offering a rationale for the almost annual hikes in lift ticket prices, and for the Skiing Corporation's aggressive search for new ski terrain in the Roaring Fork Valley and planned expansions at Buttermilk and Snowmass Resort.

In 1970 Councilman Ned Vare decided to run for the county commission seat held by Dr. J. Sterling Baxter, and Hunter Thompson, the outlaw journalist, decided to run against incumbent sheriff Carroll Whitmire. The community blew its collective cool. Conservatives said that Vare couldn't hold the offices of city councilman and county commissioner simultaneously, and that Thompson shouldn't hold the office of sheriff under any circumstances. The man admits he's an outlaw, they said, and outlaws can't be sheriffs. Thompson noted this was an honorable western tradition: the outlaw replaces his black hat with a white hat to become the leading lawman. Vare maintained that the separation of city and county governments resulted in costly duplication of services and foolish conflicts. If he served on both the council and the county commission, he would begin to forge a sensible and efficient partnership of the two. But neither Thompson's ironic logic nor Vare's reason moved Aspen residents in the fall of 1970. Before the first shots in the campaign were fired, everyone in town had taken sides. Conservatives raged, liberals cheered. Vare had already proven himself an effective official—open, innovative and concerned—and the very idea of Thompson as sheriff was compelling.

Vare's grandfather and great-uncle, Ed and Bill Vare, had ruled the city of Philadelphia and, some pols said, the state of Pennsylvania for thirty years. They were Republicans and they were bosses in the classic American tradition, and while they might have been pleased by Ned's success in the political arena, they probably would have been more comfortable with his Republican opponent, Jay Baxter.

Baxter had grown up on a Kansas farm, worked his way through medical school, married, had children, moved to Aspen, and built a successful practice. He shared offices and certain attitudes with Bugsy Barnard, had a large house in Aspen's first suburb, Snowbunny, and was the perfect picture of an American politician— burly, genial, down to earth, a master of sweet talk and shrewd moves. He cheerfully accepted the traditional political rituals and the traditional perks, was devoted to the free workings of the marketplace, and was the only Republican who'd ever been able to hold his own with Democrats Tom Sardy and Orest Gerbaz. He was popular in Aspen and well known in the county.

Ned Vare was everything a politician shouldn't be: diffident, rueful and original. Born on Philadelphia's Main Line, independently wealthy, he'd been a squash and golf champion at Yale, an architect, a teacher in several so-called free schools, and a ski instructor in Taos, New Mexico, before he moved to Aspen. A slim, balding man with fine features, Vare lived in a remodeled barn, and went around in Levi's and L. L. Bean shirts.

It would have been a classic test of Aspen's political character—the anti-pol versus the old pol, tomorrow versus yesterday—but at the last minute a third candidate entered the lists. Sam Caudill had been talked into running by people who wanted to defeat Baxter but found Vare an unacceptable alternative. Like Baxter, Caudill was a burly genial man and, like Vare, he was an architect, a liberal and a conservationist.

Vare headlined his first ad: POLITICIANS AND CON-SERVATIONISTS ARE OBSOLETE. Noting that "conservatism is valuable only when everything is perfect for everyone," Vare spoke of the folly of re-electing a conservative politician or electing "a traditional conservationist." Neither man, he said, was capable of looking forward. "We are the victims of our own success," he said, adding that the government would have to change in order to respond to the changing needs of the town.

Vare advocated a regional land use plan based on an environmental inventory, a county-wide "ecology action" program with particular emphasis on recycling and organic agriculture, a public-transit study and plan, flood plain setbacks, the removal of the Pitkin Iron Company operations, county assistance in the organization of cooperative food and medical plans, fair-cost housing for residents, an end to "exploitation of the county's working population," day-care centers for children of working mothers, national exposure of the "junk mail scandal," open meetings and "visible government," tax relief and incentives for farmers and ranchers, a master plan for the airport and creation of a "metro government" that would combine city and county offices. His campaign was low-key, his ads long thoughtful essays. The opposition, though, was not so moderate. Vare was the target of a crude mailing piece featuring a drawing depicting him as half-square, half-hippie. Titled "The Tale of the Phony Hippie," it suggested that Vare had a $2 million trust fund at Chase Manhattan Bank and referred to "King Vare and his puppets," though the "puppets" were not named. Invented quotes such as "I can play this hippie game as long as the folks' money holds out" were attributed to him.

The archetypal struggle represented in the commissioner race and the novelty of Vare's theory of city-county governance were overshadowed by the commotion that attended Thompson's candidacy. He had announced his intention to run for sheriff of Pitkin County in the October 1, 1970 issue of *Rolling Stone* magazine. It was to be, he said, the ultimate test of his anti-politics theory. His thesis, as stated in the *Aspen Wallposter,* which he and Tom Benton published for a short time, was succinct: "No doubt the Reds are Evil and the Young are Crazy, but it's hard to imagine how anybody—whatever his age or politics—could destroy this valley more efficiently than it's being destroyed by all the Right and Respectable People." His campaign symbol, designed by Benton, was a two-thumbed fist clutching a peyote button.

In his initial platform, he called for ripping up all city streets and replacing them with sod, permitting movement around the city only by foot or bicycle, changing the name of Aspen to "Fat City," installing a bastinado platform and a set of stocks in which dishonest drug dealers would be displayed on the courthouse lawn, permitting any citizen to file "a Writ of Seizure, a Writ of Stoppage, a Writ of Fear, even a Writ of Horror . . . yes . . . even a Writ of Assumption . . . against any greed-head."

Subsequently he announced plans for a comprehensive drug information program in Aspen's schools and the assignment of a nationally recognized lawman as under-sheriff. Also: the establishment of seven "action units" in the sheriff's office: a consumer action bureau, an ombudsman, a public information desk, a volunteer service corps, a legal advisory board, a police training program and a citizens' complaint department.

Thompson and Carroll Whitmire, who was seeking his second term, were joined in the fracas by former deputy sheriff Glenn Ricks. Whitmire and Ricks were like twins —both were bony and taciturn, ill-at-ease, inarticulate. Both liked all the paraphernalia of the office—fast cars, big badges, guns, cowboy hats and boots, uniforms. Both went about the business of law enforcement in the best Old West tradition. As sometimes happens with twins, they hated each other.

In a series of debates, they sat like book ends on either side of Thompson. He'd shaved his head for the occasion, and though it was a cold fall, he wore a white tennis hat, aviator glasses, khaki shorts and white sneakers. He rarely appeared without a can of beer in hand and chainsmoked, using short disposable plastic cigarette holders. Representing no tradition at all, he was articulate and garrulous. During his long discourses, in which he inevitably touched on topics as various as rock music and land development, Whitmire and Ricks stared at him as if they could not believe it was happening. At the beginning they seemed to regard Thompson's candidacy as a bad joke. Toward the end they came to fear Thompson, but though each was told by Thompson's enemies that the only way to ensure his defeat was for one of them to withdraw, neither was willing to give up. They were afraid of Thompson, but each wanted to beat the other, and each wanted the job. It only paid $10,000 a year, but it was a four-year post and a kind of power and glory went with it.

Thompson set out his philosophy in his first ad, which read in part: "The time has come it seems to dispense with all evil humor and come to grips with the strange possibility that the next sheriff of this county might very well be a foul-mouthed outlaw journalist with some very rude notions about life-styles, law enforcement and political reality in America. . . . We have come too far to back off now. . . . Aspen is ready for . . . a whole new style in government, the kind of thing Thomas Jefferson had in mind when he talked about 'democracy.' We have not done too well with that concept over the years—not in Aspen or anywhere else—and the proof of our failure is the wreckage of Jefferson's dream that haunts us on every side, from coast to coast, on the TV news and in a thousand daily newspapers. We have blown it: that fantastic possibility that Abe Lincoln called 'the last best hope of man.'

"This is the nightmare that our politicians have forced on us, even in Aspen. This valley is no longer a refuge or hideout from reality. For years, that was true. Aspen was the best of both worlds—an outpost of urban culture buried deep in the rural Rockies. It was a very salable property, as they say in show business, and for twenty years the selling orgy boomed fat and heavy.

"And now we are reaping the whirlwind—big-city problems too maligant for small-town solutions. Chicago-style traffic in a town without stoplights. Oakland-style drug busts continually bungled by simple cowboy cops who see nothing wrong with kicking handcuffed prisoners in the ribs while the sheriff stands by watching, seeing nothing wrong with it either. While the ranchers howl about zoning, New York stockbrokers and art hustlers sell this valley out from under them. The county commissioners are crude dimwit lackeys for every big-city dealer who wants a piece of the action. These rapists should be dealt with as harshly as any other criminal. This is 1970—not 1870. The powers of the sheriff's office can be focused in this direction. Why not?"

Thompson inspires no moderate emotions. Eight residents were charged with voter intimidation and conspiracy to commit voter intimidation after they allegedly attempted to discourage young Thompson supporters from registering to vote. Like Vare, Thompson was the target of an anonymous mailing piece that portrayed him as a Nazi–Hell's Angel hybrid, "Dr. Hunter Maddog Thompson, a Hell's Angel reject from Oakland." The piece claimed, "In his *Mein Kampf* (the underground *Rolling Stone*) he explains in detail how Aspen is to be made the testing ground for organized chaos, disorder and terror by a hardcore group of freaky dissenters."

At heart, Thompson didn't really want to be sheriff of Pitkin County. He just wanted to zap the greedheads and to outrage "all the Right and Respectable People." Running for sheriff was a far more outrageous and therefore more appealing and noteworthy endeavor than running for county commissioner, but the news media, including the *New York Times,* NBC and the BBC, were all covering the campaign, and Thompson's young followers believed that he was Superman, Robin Hood and the Long Ranger put together.

Thompson didn't claim to know whether he'd be a good sheriff; he didn't even claim to know what a "good sheriff " was. He just knew that Whitmire wasn't one. He knew too that, if he won and served, whether he was a good sheriff or not, he might be diminished. And if he got bored and quit, he would be diminished in another way.

He saw another danger. The blind faith of his followers might ruin him, make him soft and conceited.

For all these mixed feelings, the momentum of the campaign was building. Thompson won all the debates. An increasing number of residents found his platform sensible. Support was growing even among conservatives. His followers were tireless and passionate. In the face of all this, Thompson could not withdraw or even slow down. He had never had any talent for remaining aloof.

Given the general irrational tenor of the time, none of us was surprised when one day a man dressed in Hell's Angel colors walked into an Aspen bar, ordered a drink, stirred it with a switchblade, and asked for directions to Thompson's house. An hour later the man skidded into Thompson's driveway on a motorcycle. He claimed that he was an emissary from Sonny Barger, the chief Angel, and that on Barger's orders, Thompson would be killed and his house blown up if he won the election. The man left.

Thompson thought the emissary was a phony. The Hell's Angel colors were right, but the bike was wrong, and there were other false notes. He decided to watch the man and take no action.

Ultimately the most striking thing about the Thompson and Vare campaigns had to do not with their platforms, but with the fear and rage their candidacies generated in some residents. In the last days of the campaign, the irrational attacks on them threatened to reach a murderous level.

Five days before the election, a man from the Colorado Bureau of Investigation told Thompson that plans were under way to kill him if he won the election, but he could give him no idea who was behind the plot.

The story of the Hell's Angel surfaced about that time. After his talk with Thompson, the man disappeared for several days, only to turn up later in Thompson's campaign headquarters and announce that he'd talked with Sonny Barger again and now wanted to work for Thompson's election. The new volunteer proposed violent acts in behalf of the candidate, offering to get guns and explosives, to blow up bridges and beat up people. Thompson and his aides concluded that the man was either crazy or some sort of provocateur, took none of his suggestions, and kept watching him. Shortly thereafter an Aspen policeman told Thompson that the man was one of several undercover agents brought to Aspen by Sheriff Whitmire.

The next day Thompson and his campaign manager, Michael Solheim, confronted Whitmire, his deputy and his campaign manager in Joe Edwards's office. Deputy District Attorney James Moore arrived during the meeting.

Whitmire admitted that he had brought in a sometime federal agent, James Bromley of Englewood, Colorado, to investigate rumors involving Weathermen, bombings and other acts of violence that were being planned. He admitted too that he knew Bromley was hanging around Thompson, but claimed he'd given no orders for him to spy on Thompson or advocate violence. The sheriff repeated his story at a press conference later in the day. Bromley left town.

Even if, as some said, the Thompson campaign had begun as a joke, it ended ominously. It was as mean and ugly a time as Aspen had ever known. Though the ugliness may have been inspired by the so-called radicals, it had been manifest in the most respectable quarters in town.

In the last week of the campaign, the meanness of the moment, its terrible ironies and confusions, were demonstrated vividly when an ad signed by Fred Glidden portrayed Thompson as a kind of drug-crazed maniac who wanted to destroy the town. In more reasonable times, Glidden and Thompson would have been friends. They shared a love of literature, drink, humor and Aspen. They were both honorable men, and yet one had most dishonorably charged the other with being dishonorable. Of all the assaults, it was the only one, I think, that truly hurt Thompson. I tried to defend Glidden. I said that long ago he had taken on the role of mediator in Aspen. It was dangerous work in a town that nourished itself on extremes, and Glidden had been frequently insulted and made fun of. He loved Aspen too much and himself too little, I said. Now he's as disappointed in Aspen as he's always been in himself. He knows that all the compromises he designed for Aspen have been as ruinous as the compromises he's accepted in his own life. He can no longer be held accountable, I said, for he has been possessed by some twilight rage. Thompson understood. There was, after all, nothing but rage in Aspen that fall.

In the end, Vare lost to Baxter by a margin roughly approximate to the number of votes cast for Sam Caudill, but he won the other election. Thompson lost to Whitmire by a two-to-three margin, with Ricks a distant third. The outlaw had drawn more than 1,000 votes, but in an outlaw town, that was not so impressive.

Though Edwards and Thompson had lost, and Vare had won one and lost one, our movement grew. Others began to see it as the first clear effort since the death of Walter Paepcke to locate the true meaning of Aspen. Like Paepcke, we wanted to cherish and preserve

Aspen. But Paepcke had seen the restoration of Aspen as a human undertaking, while we saw it as a political struggle. Paepcke had revived Aspen. We wanted to slow it down. Paepcke had attempted to appeal to the people's highest instincts. We sought to expose their worst impulses. We claimed to be Paepcke's descendants, but he wanted to restore and improve a town that already was, while we wanted to do nothing less than make an Aspen that could never be along the lines of an America that never was.

DURING THOMPSON'S CAMPAIGN, the American press was bewitched by the audacity and originality of our movement. There in the heart of the mountains democracy was thriving. Hope and optimism were at work. The embarrassing American habit of putting profit and growth ahead of life itself was being challenged. America ate up this good news from the high country and came to Aspen in increasing numbers to see for itself.

At sea level the news was not good. America had begun bombing Vietcong supply routes in Cambodia. The fighting had spread to Laos as well as Cambodia. Lieutenant William Calley was found guilty by the courts, but much of the nation treated him like a hero. Louis Armstrong and Audie Murphy died. Rock impresario Bill Graham closed the Fillmores East and West. President Nixon ordered a freeze on wages and prices in an effort to curb inflation and strengthen the American balance of payments position. Sixty people were killed in a California earthquake. Amtrak took over the country's passenger trains. Ten guards and thirty-two prisoners were killed during a revolt at Attica prison. A farm labor contractor was charged in the murders of twenty people in northern California. *Look* magazine died. The "Jesus

Movement" burgeoned. A new play by Edward Albee opened on Broadway. It was called *All Over.*

In Aspen we had faith that once runaway growth was controlled, life would be beautiful for everyone again. We assumed that we had the power to control growth. We had lost elections but won power, and we could not be stopped. Mayor Eve Homeyer said in 1971, "It's time we stopped feeling guilty about promoting the town and realize that it's legal and moral to sell a good product." We pushed harder. In petitions, screeds and letters to public officials, we said that Aspen was more than a product. It was a place with its own integrity, its own imperatives. We demanded more from both the city and county governments: more stringent zoning in both the city and county, a public transit system, parking structures, a mall in downtown Aspen—all of the things that the Master Plan had called for. There seemed to be more of us, and we had become skillful in the tactics of government by petition.

The town squared off in 1972 for an Olympic debate. Denver had been chosen as the site for the 1976 winter Olympic games, and the Denver Olympics Committee and the Aspen Skiing Corporation directors had privately agreed that the alpine events would be held in Aspen. When the town learned of the agreement, it divided quickly and sharply. Mayor Homeyer announced she would oppose Aspen's participation in the Olympics with all of her strength. Elizabeth Paepcke, too, argued eloquently against the games, reminding the city council that her husband had rejected the games twenty years earlier for fear they would trigger a ruinous boom. Her position put her at odds with her brother, Paul Nitze, the principal Skiing Corporation stockholder. Snowmass Resort and the Aspen Chamber of Commerce pushed for the games. We fought back. The debate in the Pitkin County Courthouse was long, noisy, acrimonious. Despite her vow, Mrs. Homeyer capitulated early. The council was split.

The Denver Olympics Committee backed off and eliminated Aspen from its plans before any formal decision was made. The fight, however, was taken up across the state. The 1972 election ballot included a referendum question: Should the 1976 winter Olympics be held in Colorado? Data from previous Olympics sites indicated that though a few profited, the public costs— social as well as financial—were staggering. Colorado voters rejected the Olympics, thoroughly embarrassing the Denver barons who had made and won the bid. We in Aspen claimed credit for beating our own pols, the Skiing Corporation and Denver in one move. Our vision was clearly paramount.

14∧
The Politics of Innocence

THE PROSPECTORS did not battle with the Indians in the Roaring Fork Valley in 1879. In the 1950s those who objected to Paepcke's platonic notion of Aspen confined their complaints to cocktail party japery. In the 1960s, the out-of-town developers overtook Aspen as easily as the snow overtakes the mountains. In the Edwards campaign of 1969 and the Thompson and Vare campaigns of 1970, direct assault was met by dirty tricks and dark plots. In the 1972 election the battle would be finally joined.

On both sides the partisans had grown bold. On both sides there was great energy and dedication, and a degree of madness. In one corner, along with conservatives, were the blood descendants of the prospectors, all the developers and speculators, would-be merchant princes and land barons, boomers and hustlers, libertarians and people who liked to say, "It's a free country." In the other corner, along with liberals, were the Indians' self-annointed heirs, the noble savages and environmentalists, anarchists, sentimentalists, dopers and vegetarians, fading flower children, saviors of wolves and assorted radicals. There were good people on each side, there were righteous people, and there were bad guys.

It seemed an even match. When the dust had settled, the Roaring Fork Valley would have decisively settled the old American question: are we here for love or money?

The moment was at hand, but Thompson, Vare and I were on the sidelines. Having lost his city council seat to a conservative and his taste for battle, Vare had moved to a ranch near Silt, Colorado, sixty miles from Aspen. Thompson was on the road, covering the 1972 Presidential campaign, the subject of his third book, *Fear and Loathing: On the Campaign Trail '72*. I had said to Thompson one night, "Every problem does not have a political solution," and left the arena forever.

The movement in which we once played central roles did not miss us. With the backing of the Citizens for Community Action, Joe Edwards and his law partner and close friend Dwight Shellman ran for the county commission. Slight, darkly handsome, Edwards was an angry candidate, railing against the fatcats, noting the damage they had done and would go on doing to the place if they were not checked. He proposed stern measures to stop runaway growth, and pastoral measures to restore the small town that had got lost in the boom. Shellman, fair, scholarly, was the whiz kid as pol. He presented himself as the best and the brightest. Part philosopher, part technician, he was precise, calm, certain.

In the general election, Democratic Presidential candidate George McGovern took Pitkin County ("Pitkin County and Massachusetts," someone said), and Edwards and Shellman took the Pitkin County Courthouse. Edwards easily won a three-way race, succeeding Tom Sardy, who had decided to retire after more than two decades as commissioner. Shellman whipped incumbent Clyde Vagneur, a rancher from a pioneer family. When the two new men took their seats at the commissioners' table, the New Politics overtook the county. With or without cooperation from the third commissioner, Jay Baxter, the two young activists could work their will on the county.

The dynamic duo. Edwards-and-Shellman. Shellman-and-Edwards. For a time people spoke of them as one person, but they were quite different. Edwards was a kind of poet, Shellman a kind of mechanic. They were complementary but different.

When Edwards spoke of Aspen, he spoke quietly but passionately. He loved it all and wanted to preserve it all —rivers, meadows, forests, vast ranches, small town. He had enormous expectations for the place. Shellman, on the other hand, could not resist tinkering with the machinery, whether it was the county buses or the county itself, in his desire to make something better, or failing that, something different. Most of all, he was in love with his own notion of things, his own cleverness. He couldn't help embellishing, tampering, fine-tuning, taking the county apart and putting it back together again in a more interesting way, his way. He had enormous ambitions for himself.

Another outspoken opponent of growth, Stacy Standley, a young bartender turned ski area consultant, succeeded Mrs. Homeyer as mayor of Aspen in May 1973. Tall, gangly, open-faced, Standley looked like a farm boy but functioned like a technician.

Three bright young men were running Aspen, but a gang of mean old pols was still running the nation. Though five men rumored to be employed by the Nixon campaign organization were arrested in Democratic National Headquarters, Nixon and his Vice-president, Spiro Agnew, were re-elected in a near-record landslide. On the eve of the election Henry Kissinger said, "Peace is at hand," but it wasn't. America was mining North Vietnamese ports. The Dow-Jones average topped 1000 for the first time, but the fuel shortage began to surface. There was evidence that an ITT contribution to Nixon's campaign had resulted in a Justice Department settlement of an antitrust suit in favor of the conglomerate.

Three months after Nixon's second inauguration, the Watergate saga began to unfold. A number of top aides resigned. Former attorney general John Mitchell and others were indicted. The Senate Watergate hearings were a TV hit. There was talk of impeachment. Agnew had his own Watergate and resigned.

Saigon fell. The few remaining Americans there fled. Despite Nixon's claim of achieving "peace with honor," the war continued. Fifty-six thousand Americans and millions of Vietnamese were killed between 1965 and 1973. One hundred and nine billion dollars was spent, and when it was over, no one seemed to know why.

The dollar was devalued again. The Arab oil embargo triggered an energy crisis, and thousands of Americans lost their jobs as a result. *The Godfather* was named best motion picture of the year.

Things couldn't have been worse in America; things couldn't have been better in Aspen. The city fathers held in abeyance all building permits in potential conflict with a pending tightening of city zoning regulations. They also passed a plan for a mall in downtown Aspen, and purchased a large tract of land between the Jerome and the Roaring Fork River. The commissioners rezoned the entire county. The liberals and preservationists beamed; the burghers were too busy to complain. Business boomed as Americans in increasing numbers sought the Great Escape in Aspen. Plans went forward simultaneously for a $5 million hospital, an $850,000 solar-heated airport terminal, the $1 million mall and a $10 million light-rail transit line between Aspen and Snowmass Resort. An elaborate system of trails and parks was also in the works.

There were some unhappy people. Real estate firms lobbied against the city's tighter zoning. Landowners in the county reacted to the more stringent zoning in the county with lawsuits totaling $32 million. Woody Creek ranchers, who objected to both the new constraints on their land and the proposed light-rail system, mounted a recall effort against the new commissioners. But these efforts came to nothing because Aspen had begun a whole new game, with new rules and new imperatives.

Like the prospectors, Paepcke and the sixties developers, the New Pols took the place with no real opposition. There were arguments, but they were not about meanings. They were about money. The problem was not that restrictive zoning was philosophically abhorrent as an abridgement of individual rights, but that zoning might lower the value of the land. It was not that the million-dollar mall might destroy the fine flinty character of downtown Aspen by glossing it over with the thin chic of a shopping center, but that it might discourage shoppers by forcing them to walk an extra block or two. It was not that the network of trails and parks would diminish the wilderness instead of restoring it, but that it was expensive and excluded cars. The lobbying, the lawsuits, the recall threat seemed reflexive responses, vestiges of an Old West sensibility that was rapidly becoming obsolete.

But if the burghers lacked some fine philosophical passion, it was lacking too in the New Pols. From the moment they took office, Dwight Shellman, Joe Edwards and Stacy Standley seemed to lack Vare and Thompson's sense of both the problems and the stakes. Like many lawyers, Shellman and Edwards proved better games-men than advocates, and ski area consultant Standley seemed to get his wisdom from the computer. For all their bold moves, Shellman, Edwards and Standley focused on the legal rather than philosophical issues. They said, in effect, "We can do this, and therefore we will." Though they were true believers in the anti-growth cause, it was apparent by the end of 1973 that they were as incapable as their predecessors of strug-gling with the gut issues, of articulating the deepest con-cerns of their supporters or answering the serious ques-tions raised by a few conservatives. They spoke of their "mandate" and proceeded to carry it out, but they never actually defined it; and so the long struggle between commerce and nature in Aspen was reduced to natter-ing about dollars and cents.

As they worked their will on Aspen, Shellman, Ed-wards and Standley made it clear that they thought they could do anything, have everything. Though they were Aspen's most devoted stewards since Paepcke, their vi-sion of the place probably would have been unrecogniz-able to him. It was at once grander and more ambitious, and more sentimental. It was pure American. Paepcke had known that limits were essential. Aspen could be a lovely town where art and sport were celebrated and businessmen were radicalized in the true sense of the word, but it could not be more than that. Shellman, Edwards and Standley recognized no such limits. Aspen could be whatever they wanted it to be. Whatever it had been, their actions suggested, it would now be better, freer and more beautiful than any town had ever been.

It would be a new kind of place, unprecedented, in which everyone could realize his aspirations—as long, that is, as his aspirations were not at odds with the official aspirations.

ERHARD SEMINAR TRAINING (est) and Aspen were made for each other. Aspen was the capital of hubris; est was its ministry. When Werner Erhard said, we are each and every one of us perfect, he found a large and agreeable congregation in Aspen.

Erhard, a used-car dealer from eastern Pennsylvania who one day left his car lot and his family, changed his name and moved to San Francisco, had assembled the tenets of est in the way that IBM assembles typewriters. In the early 1970s he became Aspen's leading guru, turning up regularly to conduct his weekend sessions.

Aspen was peculiarly susceptible to gurus, but it seemed a long slide from Paepcke to Erhard. Paepcke said that we were perfectible. Erhard said we were perfect just the way we were. Paepcke believed that we owed service to our fellow man. Erhard, taking Philip Slater's irony straight, said each of us was alone on the continent and had absolute rights in our own "space." Paepcke believed that if we dedicated a lifetime to the search, we might begin to understand life's mysteries. Erhard said we could "get it" in one weekend at the Holiday Inn.

Est hit Aspen like an epidemic. Someone would joke about est one week, take it the next week, become one of Erhard's apostles the week after that. A woman told me that Erhard ranked right up there with Jung and Freud. A holdout said she felt cowardly for not taking est. A rich est graduate told a poor non-est grad that people who worried about money would always be poor. Friendships, marriages, love affairs ended or began over est.

Dwight Shellman and Joe Edwards took est and found it so valuable that they urged all county employees to take the training. They said that the county would pay half the cost. Many residents, including some of the staunchest supporters of Shellman and Edwards, were furious and baffled by this violation of the principle of separation of church and state. Many county workers did take advantage of the offer, and the courthouse became a temple of perfection. In response to a column critical of the downtown mall, Edwards wrote a lengthy letter accusing me of having been brainwashed by Barnard, and of opposing my old political allies simply for the sake of opposing them. That, he suggested, was the way of journalists. The New Politics seemed to have vanished only moments after it had been officially sanctioned by the voters of Pitkin County.

It could not be said with any conviction that Shellman, Edwards and Standley did in the New Politics by themselves. It could not even be said that they took more power than we meant them to have, or that they violated their campaign promises. They used the power we gave them to do what they said they would do, and they did it very fast. In that sense they were perfect leaders, and rare ones.

The essential problem had to do with the character of Aspen and the character of America. At bottom, the people of Aspen have always believed the town was special, unique and therefore capable of achievements beyond lesser places. Aspen people have always believed that they were superior to other people—luckier, smarter and more capable—and that they could get away with things other people couldn't get away with. This superiority complex, this eternal hubris, was at no time more visible than it was during the first years of the Shellman-Edwards-Standley reign. At the same time America was suffering a national failure of nerve. Everything that could go wrong seemed to be going wrong. The country had lost a war. Its leaders were going to jail. Its children were mocking it. The economy was faltering. But Aspen, God, Aspen was up there—sassy, stylish, sound and happy. America was worried about money and power; Aspen was concerned with saving the forests and preserving the streams. Americans were saving money; Aspen residents were saving their souls. And so America said, Man, they got it made in Aspen. This adulation was not lost on Aspen. Its superiority complex grew. New Politics was gone, but it was replaced by Now Politics. Do it now. Go for it.

NOW POLITICS is about means, not ends. There is only the moment, and the moment is Now, and we must make the most of it. But this obsession with means, this ignorance of ends, can backfire. On paper the means looked right, but in practice, they worked badly. Shellman and Edwards promised to slow down growth, to defuse the boom and to restore the serenity and pastoral ambience of the place. Their means seemed sensible and logical. They tightened and extended zoning throughout the county. In areas where literally thousands of houses might have been built, the construction of only a few hundred houses was permitted under the stringent new regulations. The old zoning permitted one house on every quarter-acre. In some cases, the new zoning required thirty acres per house.

Growth was slowed dramatically, but land prices rose

rapidly. By limiting the supply of available land, the commissioners had unwittingly increased the demand. Fewer houses were built, but they were more expensive houses. Speculators, developers, contractors and construction workers continued to prosper. As the supply continued to decline, the demand continued to rise, along with prices. Residents, unless they were rich, could not afford to buy land in Pitkin County. Real estate brokers and speculators, the very people Shellman and Edwards meant to control, were the chief beneficiaries. Naturally, as the impact of tighter zoning in the city was felt, prices on existing houses and condominiums rose too.

Shellman, Edwards and Standley set out to return Aspen and the valley to its residents, to take it away from the developers and speculators, but instead they turned it over to part-time residents who could, and apparently would, pay almost anything for a piece of land, a house or a condominium in Aspen.

Their efforts to restore the small-town flavor to the place backfired in the same way. The means—legislation of green space around the edge of the city, creation of parks and a mall in the city, construction of trails throughout the more populated sections of the county, mandatory design approval of everything from new buildings to new signs—seemed reasonable. But no genuine American small town has a mall, parks, trails. It can't afford such embellishments and doesn't need them because the woods are nearby and accessible. Nor do most genuine small towns exercise design control over every new building or sign: this would be considered an infringement of individual rights. Once all these elements were in place, Aspen came to resemble not a sweet small town, but a rigid regulated resort. However salutary in theory, and however pleasant the parks, trails, mall, tasteful buildings and graphics, this obsession with surfaces made Aspen look like a big, successful, bland pleasure dome. A resident said, "They said they were going to give the town back to us, but they turned it into a God damn cruise ship."

The mall epitomized the gap between theory and fact, means and end. It was a nice idea, a mall—"a people place," according to its proponents. Cars would be kept out; trees, bushes and flowers brought in. There might be benches, tables, sculptures. It would be very tasteful. During a Design Conference, a block was made into a temporary mall. The designers were pleased. Residents seemed to like it too. On a couple of Earth Days, the nation's annual observance of environmental concerns, streets were blocked off again. High school students polled passersby, most of whom thought it was nice. Finally a group of high school students submitted a mall petition to the city council. Their lawyer was Joe Edwards, who at that time was still in private practice. Judging by the number of signatures, the eloquence of the students and the legal persuasiveness of Edwards, the mall was an idea whose time had come. The petitioners said, in effect, "You can do this yourselves, or we will go over your heads to the people, and it will be done anyway." Its inception was a triumph of New Politics, but its creation, was a Now Politics achievement.

Three blocks forming a "U" in the heart of downtown Aspen were designated the mall. One million dollars was budgeted for its construction. After a vigorous design debate, the most sylvan design was chosen. The mall's surface would be paved with 350,000 serrated liver-colored bricks from St. Louis. A man-made stream would run down the center of one leg of the mall. Grass would be set on either side of the stream, along with flowers and trees. There would be tasteful benches, streetlights and trash containers. Dogs would not be permitted in the mall. In the summer, restaurants would have tables and chairs in the mall. Street musicians and magicians would perform there, and people would sit about and watch the passing parade. There would be a timber jungle gym for kids. There might eventually be a bandstand and a fountain. It was done.

On one level, it worked. Even merchants who had feared that the mall was equivalent to bankruptcy for them found their business growing. Tourists loved the mall, as it turned out. Street musicians also found it more profitable than the streets, and people who worked in downtown Aspen found it pleasant to gather there at lunchtime. It immediately became an integral part of the town's promotional campaigns, a staple post-card and ad shot. It photographed beautifully and made Aspen look serene, lovely, like a kind of wonderland. People said to each other, "I'm going to the mall this afternoon," as if they were actually going someplace. As a means of reducing automobile traffic, encouraging pedestrians, reducing air pollution and giving downtown Aspen a serene small-town air, it worked.

But there were some problems. The St. Louis bricks were hard to keep clear of snow, so treacherous icy patches frequently caused pedestrians to slip and fall. The man-made stream was sometimes dry, other times a flood. Since no cars were permitted there, the streets around the mall were more congested than ever. Emergency vehicles were permitted to enter the mall, but wheeling through its elaborate appointments was hard, firemen said. All deliveries to businesses on the mall had to be made via alleys that were sometimes impassable.

There were more serious problems. The price of commercial space on the mall skyrocketed. A small store there rented for about $5,000 a month in 1979. There once was a mix of enterprises on the mall—exotic restaurants, elegant shops, down-to-earth stores and simple cafés where hardhats gathered for coffee and doughnuts. Now it has become the precinct of haute schlock—expensive boutiques and quaint restaurants. The more ordinary businesses have been priced out. The White Kitchen, a favorite locals' hangout for forty years, went out of business about a year after the mall opened.

There is something unreal about the stores and restaurants on the mall, and there is something unreal about the mall itself. It isn't ugly, but it isn't Aspen as old-timers remember it either. It is less Aspen restored than Aspen revised. The Now Politicians boast about the mall. This, they say, is what we can do. Standley once said that anyone who didn't like the mall probably didn't belong in Aspen. Adherents of the mall—residents, part-time residents and tourists—agree. But the older residents—people born in Aspen and now in their sixties or seventies—see the mall as foolish, inconvenient, even ominous. One older woman said, "I'm afraid of it. I wouldn't go in there on a bet." A sturdy profane woman whose husband was killed in the mines fifty years ago, she still hauls her own coal. She is proud, independent and afraid of no one, but she is afraid of the mall and walks around it rather than through it. She used to know those streets as well as she knew the shape of her own hands, but now she doesn't know them and doesn't like them, and thinks "terrible things go on there, terrible people are there, crazy people."

In fact nothing terrible goes on in the mall. But in trying to bring the country into the city, the pols somehow sullied both the country and the city. By trying to make Aspen both, they made it neither. One can walk from downtown Aspen to the real country—the forest and the river—in five minutes, but few people do anymore. The real country is forgot, and the real town has become unreal, more a movie set than a place. That is why an old woman who has lived in Aspen for seventy-five years feels like an alien in her home town, and why tourists feel more and more at home there.

AMERICANS HAVE ALWAYS been better at nostalgia than at anticipation. We love cowboys, dead Presidents and the music we grew up with. We long for the good old days when coffee was 5 cents a cup, when men were men and people were nice and the grass was greener. Americans cannot resist the new and the novel, but at heart we are obsessed with our past—meaning our youth, our promise. We endlessly chase frontiers in the belief that out there, it is still fresh, still chaste. For thirty-five years John Wayne was the embodiment of our most constant idea. He was an actor, then a star, then a hero and finally an idea, because he symbolized a time when America was still the good guy. We like symbols better than facts.

Shellman, Edwards and Standley, along with many other residents, saw Aspen as a symbol and not a fact, and set about to re-create the frontier. Looking back for inspiration at a West that never was, an Aspen that never was, they passed ordinance after ordinance designed to legislate the good old days into being. Saying that the valley should remain open and green and wild as it had been in the decades preceding the boom, they tightened zoning regulations. Now, they said, ranchers can work their land in peace. But ranching had always been a marginal activity at that altitude and in that climate, and the ranchers were tired of it. They could sell the land they had been slaves to and be rich and idle. The commissioners drove the prices up and the ranchers began to sell. Expensive modern houses now dot that once open, green, wild prospect.

In the same way, Shellman, Edwards and Standley wanted to re-create the small town with such pastoral touches as the mall, the parks, the trails. It was a nostalgic exercise that had little to do with the facts. The facts were that Aspen had been a rough mining camp, a booming city and a dying place, in *that* order. When Walter Paepcke arrived, he made it into a gathering place for the best and the brightest. Aspen had never been the sweet small town that Shellman, Edwards and Standley were trying to re-create.

Out in the county, where they meant to preserve the wilderness, they made instead an expensive preserve for affluent Americans. In Aspen itself, they replaced an old commercial district with a kind of hip shopping center. They meant to cool the boom and re-create the small town, but they refueled the boom and made a chic watering hole.

Their intentions were good. Their means, however vehement, were conventional. When growth is too rapid, you tighten up zoning to slow it down. When there are too many cars and too much commotion, you install a mall. When a place becomes too urban, you make parks and trails. When you are threatened by people with bad taste, you legislate good taste. But the plan went awry.

Affluent Americans, along with dreamy young people, flocked to Aspen in greater numbers than ever before. According to the 1966 Master Plan projections, the county would have 22,000 tourist beds by 1985. Aspen was already ten years ahead of itself. There were 22,000 tourist beds by 1975, and much of the winter and occasionally in summer, all of those beds were filled. At those times, the little mountain town was as crowded and hectic as midtown Manhattan during rush hour. But crowds were only part of the problem. More bothersome to many residents was the increasing emphasis on money and fashion. Aspen had always been above commerce, but suddenly it was rich and chic. The pols had meant to make utopia and they had made a bonanza. Hunter Thompson's notion of "a town where people could live like human beings instead of slaves to some bogus sense of Progress" had a certain poignancy.

That, of course, is the trouble with confusing symbols and facts. Aspen was a fact, America was a fact, but facts are messier than symbols and tougher to deal with. They cannot be made into something they are not. Shellman, Edwards, Standley and their supporters tried to legislate symbols: the frontier, the small town. But the facts of life in Aspen, of America intruded. When supply decreases, demand increases. When prices rise, the rich play a larger role than the poor. When a place grows prettier, it becomes more popular. When commerce and nature combine, they combine rudely. When you say you are a symbol, you are generally believed. In a country obsessed with its lost innocence, any place that looks innocent—fresh, spirited, youthful—will attract crowds.

Burdened with the double disgrace of Vietnam and Watergate, in the grip of a serious recession, guilt-ridden and exhausted, America in the mid-seventies was a sad and sorry place. But Aspen was booming, sassy and vigorous. The party seemed to be over in America, but it was on in Aspen, and the Now Pols were most indulgent hosts.

Whatever they meant to make, they had made a pretty arena in which pleasure was the principal commodity. The pastoral pleasures of wide meadows inhabited by fat cows and healthy horses, parks set like manicured wilderness in the townscape, meandering trails, endless open prospects that had been legislated into being. The more urgent pleasures of art and sport that had been handed down from the Paepcke era. The new pleasures to be found in exotic, and usually illegal, chemicals. The pleasures of narcissism available in a plethora of such so-called consciousness-raising rites as est and the pleasures of the free and easy way of life mandated by those rites.

The pleasure principle made Aspen, according to the *Los Angeles Times,* "THE place of the seventies." The Aspen way of life was more profitable than silver or snow, culture or development. In his campaigns, Joe Edwards had said flatly that residents could "sell or save" Aspen. He had set out to "save" it, but in focusing so singlemindedly on the means, Edwards did not see that the inevitable end: Aspen was moving into absolute sync with affluent America.

Early in his term, he decided it would be a wonderful thing if people could ride their horses into Aspen and leave them in a clean, well-lit stable while they did their errands. He ordered the Pitkin County Stable to be built near the courthouse. It had a fine view of Smuggler Mountain, got the morning sun, but except for Edwards's own horse, it was virtually unoccupied. Some young people complained that the stable was nicer than their own digs. Conservatives raged that Edwards had spent $10,000 of public money to stable his horse. Both the young people and the conservatives missed the point. There was neither thoughtlessness nor selfishness in his act, only the most extraordinary nostalgia.

By trying to go back to a time that never was, the Now Politicians moved Aspen into the very heart of the present; for in the seventies America's search for its lost innocence had become an obsession. Now Politics could also be called the politics of innocence.

15 ∧
Good Times, Bad Times

IN 1974 AMERICA suffered inflation, rising fuel prices, a lag in economic growth, a plummeting Dow-Jones average: in short, a severe recession. Gasoline was in short supply, but profits of four major oil companies were up nearly 100 percent. Patty Hearst and the Symbionese Liberation Army were in the headlines. As White House aides went to jail one by one and the House of Representatives moved toward impeaching President Nixon, he resigned. Vice President Gerald R. Ford assumed the Presidency; one of his first acts was the granting of a full pardon to Nixon. The Oscar-winning movie for 1974 was *The Sting.*

But 1974 was a very good year for Aspen. Business was good. There was plenty of snow and there were plenty of jobs. Real estate prices continued to rise because there were still more buyers than sellers. Pitkin County hadn't much liked Nixon anyway, and the new President was a Vail man. But we had mixed feelings about our success. On one hand, Aspen seemed impervious to national trauma, above it all. On the other, our success was embarrassing and confusing. We had done all the things towns do to control their own destinies, had applied all the traditional brakes to the boom, but the boom was as impervious to our efforts as Aspen was to the nation's ills.

The houses of long-time residents were becoming increasingly valuable. Even old ski bums like Joan and Shady Lane, whose aversion to success was famous in Aspen, who had conscientiously avoided all the roads that lead to riches, were getting rich. The Lanes' land, with its old houses and barns casually scavenged through the years, was worth hundreds of thousands of dollars. Joan Lane began wintering in Paris. Somehow Aspen had become one of those legendary places that people talk about, visit, love. For all its erratic history, its eccentricities, its startling dives and climbs, Aspen was playing the all-American game better than America itself. We didn't know what to make of it.

By the 1970s American businessmen not only understood the American mood, but exploited it. Rocked by assassinations, war, street turmoil and inflation, the American people sought new diversions, and business led the search.

The so-called hippies or flower children still frightened our leaders and other conservatives, but businessmen recognized the enormous merchandising possibilities and profit in their way of life. The flower children had slipped the bonds of puritanism. They suggested that freedom, joy and youth were available to everyone. At bottom their rebellion seemed so . . . sensible. War *was* hell, after all. Taxes were a bore. Sex was fun. What was once forbidden was now nearly mandatory. The revolution was a party to which nearly everyone eventually came.

Except for the very conservative, everyone joined in. Allen Ginsberg, the beatnik poet of the fifties, had a small audience and many critics. Allen Ginsberg, the high priest of the flower children, had an enormous audience and many fans. *Easy Rider,* a movie that celebrated drugs and condemned the American Dream, was a great success and led to a succession of movies that portrayed the young as heroes and their elders as villains. Blue jeans were seen as often on Madison Avenue as they were in Harvard Square. In their boots and ethnic garb, suburban matrons began to resemble some new breed of peasants. Rock 'n' roll became the dominant music. Bob Dylan was everyone's hero. Bean sprouts turned up in Park Avenue kitchens as well as Berkeley pads. Politicians began wearing their hair longer and their attitudes looser. The dream merchants offered $50 designer jeans, "natural" breakfast cereals, more varieties of rock than Chuck Berry could imagine, young TV and movie stars, everything to make a sad old nation feel young and happy again.

Aspen had been one of the original rebel encampments, pre-dating this national celebration of youth by more than a decade. In the seventies the town offered itself up to the nation's sunshine rebels. Aspen businesses and local government seemed to be finally allied.

Fifteen years earlier, Aspen businesses had been straightforward enterprises—Aspen Sports, Valley Kilns, Alpine Jewelers, the Aspen Bookshop were typical. By the seventies there was another kind of business too. Peaches En Regalia, Run for Your Life, The Inside Job, Therapy, Entropy purported to sell not mere merchandise but the Aspen way of life itself. The way was "laid back," mellow, cool, fast, easy, narcissistic. The way was hedonism, and the nation was grateful for it. It became very profitable, with its $50 prefaded, preshrunk, tightly cut bell-bottom denim jeans from France, $100 embroidered shirts, boots, sheepskin vests, beads, rings, bangles, "natural" hair, mega-vitamins, vegetarian foods, wheat germ lasagna, stained-glass windows to order, incense, hanging plants, candles, tee shirts with a message, TM, est, arica and the "human potential" movement.

Coming and going as casually as the tourists, Aspen shops in the 1970s seemed to eschew such traditional goals of retailing as reliable service and constancy, and resembled small temples of "higher consciousness" in which customers are treated as novitiates, possibly salvagable. In Aspen, tourists are called "turkeys" by residents, who call themselves "locals." It is a wonderful thing to be perceived as a "local," and there is always the possibility that if a turkey spends enough time and money in these marts of "higher consciousness," he will become . . . a local.

America's disillusionment with itself after the sound and fury of the 1960s and the whiplashes of the early 1970s was understandable. The revolution had failed, the Establishment had failed. The Communists had completed their takeover of South Vietnam and South Vietnamese refugees began to arrive in America. Ugly facts about CIA activities in this country and overseas were revealed. The FBI, after spending millions of dollars, finally caught Patty Hearst. Twice, women tried to assassinate President Ford. Cambodia captured a U.S. merchant ship, the *Mayaguez*. We sent in the Marines, bombed a Cambodian air base and retrieved the ship. The nation applauded: it was the first battle we'd won in a long time.

After the pain came the search for pleasure. Pleasure in Aspen was so, well, upright. Skiing was healthy and challenging. Concerts were inspiring. Institute lectures were informative. The townscape and countryside were clean and stylish.

Politicians, developers, rebels, burghers, idealists,

hedonists, residents and visitors—everyone demanded more of everything from Aspen. More profits, more pastoral prospects, more beauty, more efficiency, more pleasure, more security. The unceasing pressure of all those divergent aspirations converged, and the burghers' long-held belief in their absolute right to prosper blended so smoothly with the rebels' absolute right to live as they wished that one could not tell where one stopped and the other began.

Our confusion grew. We understood less and less. Something was happening to Aspen, and something was happening to us, but we didn't know what it was. We had our irises read, chewed roots, jogged, did graduate work in est as if we were preparing for a battle. But it wasn't clear who the enemy was. The conservatives had betrayed us. The liberals had screwed up. It was hard to tell the difference between Old Politics, New Politics and Now Politics. Having ruined itself, America had come to Aspen to ruin it. But perhaps the enemy was us.

On January 1, 1976 there were more people on the mountains, in town and on the streets than there had ever been. They kept coming. But the crowds were forgot in late March when singer-actress Claudine Longet shot and killed pro skier Vladimir "Spider" Sabich in the house they shared in Starwood, the exclusive subdivision celebrated by John Denver in his song, "Starwood in Aspen." The killing received international attention.

Accompanied by her former husband, singer Andy Williams, Longet appeared in court and testified that Sabich had been showing her how to use a .22 pistol when it accidentally went off and killed him. She was charged with reckless manslaughter. An English journalist said, "Aspen is not a nice place." He said the shooting could not have occurred anywhere but Aspen, suggesting that it was silly, childish, clumsy, a crime of hedonism, not passion. Aspen residents were angry at Longet —some because she killed a hero, some because she turned a harsh spotlight on Aspen. The resultant bad press might damage Aspen's reputation or cut into business. Other people were angry at the press for presuming to judge Aspen, analyze it. Judgment had lost favor in Aspen.

There was more bad news in the fall. By Thanksgiving there was so little snow on the ground that the lifts couldn't open. It was clear by mid-December that one of the droughts that occasionally afflict the West had hit. Endless sunny, dry days scorched the mountains and western plains, while snow fell in unprecedented amounts in the Northeast. For the first time in modern history, the winter did not draw throngs of skiers to Aspen. Christmas was not merry. The Aspen Skiing Corporation estimated that it lost $4 million over the holidays. The number of jobless mounted in Aspen. Bureaucrats came to town to offer food stamps, government-subsidized jobs and low-interest business loans. Ski area operators raged when Colorado Senator Floyd Haskell suggested the mountains be declared a disaster area. Ski men said it would ruin their "image." The Aspen Community Church set up a soup kitchen, and the Reverend Paul Harvey announced that he would fast until snow came. People who knew the history of the place remembered that the last time the place had fallen this far this fast, it had taken fifty years to recover.

There was nothing happy about the new year. The snow drought got worse and Claudine Longet's trial got under way. TV networks, every major newspaper and news magazine sent reporters to Aspen. Sensational images of an immoral, decadent and *snowless* Aspen flashed around the world. The jury finally found Longet guilty of a lesser charge, negligent homicide, and sentenced her to thirty days in jail. The press found Aspen guilty of hedonism. America's ardor for Aspen only increased.

BY THE SPRING the drought was awful to see. For the first time in all my years in the valley, it was showing its age. In that suddenly stale and dusty place, I finally understood the meaning of the West. As wise men have always said, it is a desert before and after it is anything else. Only chance, luck and good weather—meaning snow in the mountains—hold the desert at bay.

In that brittle hot landscape it was impossible to go on pretending that we had absolute dominion over the valley. One dry winter had not only left the valley shrunken and sad, it had turned back legions of tourists, thwarted all the people with big ideas, and shown that everything is as transient as the weather itself. I would like to claim that this new understanding of mine was a manifestation of wisdom. It wasn't. It was merely a tardy recognition of the facts of the place.

There are moments when all that is the valley peaks in a crescendo of sights and sounds, when its essence is suddenly visible, almost palpable. That essence has only to do with the place.

The valley extends so far back through time that it is impossible to imagine its beginnings. The mountains rose through processes logical only to geologists, and the valley has not changed at all. Aspen is there, and Snowmass and Woody Creek and Emma and Basalt and Carbondale and Snowmass Resort, but they are merely dots in a vastness that stretches far beyond our capacity to understand.

Before 1879 the Utes inhabited the valley. They were crowded out by the prospectors, who were followed by merchants and whores and railroad men and tycoons. They all blew it. After World War II scholars and rogues came into the valley. They were followed by sporting men and fancy ladies and developers and burghers and rebels. From time to time one feels the surge of all that has gone before, and that surge blows away all the boundaries and knocks down all the walls we have carefully erected. In the presence of dinosaurs, Indians, prospectors, whores, tycoons, scholars, rogues and developers, one sees that there is only one constant: the valley itself. One sees that it knows more about preserving and restoring itself than all the generations of people who have inhabited it.

The drought's effects on the valley were terrible, but passing. Its effects on the people were terrible, and permanent. The drought was seen as an affront, an outrage, a crime of nature that would not go unpunished. Townspeople set about to ensure against any further natural blunders against anything that might threaten their dominion.

The Aspen Skiing Corporation announced plans to install expensive and elaborate snowmaking equipment at Buttermilk and later on Aspen Mountain. The weather had failed them only once in thirty-one years, but once was too much. In late February 1977, a "weather modification" firm was hired by Aspen, several other mountain towns and the state of Colorado to seed clouds over the mountains. The effectiveness of cloud-seeding and its long-term effects remain unclear, but the process is a wonderful way of giving the finger to Mother Nature. There had been no clouds to seed until late February because of a kink in the westerlies, the winds that normally carry Pacific storms across the central Rockies. That winter though, they'd been driven north into Canada and then south into New England. The moment the clouds arrived, the seeding operation got under way. When the snow began to fall, the seeders took full credit for it. A few people suggested that cloud-seeding was at least unnatural and perhaps environmentally hazardous, but they were shouted down by the people who crowed that Aspen had prevailed again. Comedian Buddy Hackett, a part-time Aspen resident, flew some of the new Aspen snow to Hollywood and showed it to the nation on "The Tonight Show."

After a wetter summer than usual and a balmy fall, snows came in November 1977 in depths that had not been seen in the Roaring Fork Valley in a decade. Aspen claimed further credit. The snow wiped out the effects of the drought on the valley, but the people had been permanently marked. They had been badly frightened, but they had beat the weather, and made the feat more than it was in the way that a cowboy who breaks one stallion to halter thinks he has broken the world itself to halter. The fear faded. The valley, its integrity, its imperatives, receded from their minds. America itself seemed to be receding.

The 1976 American Bicentennial celebration was a solemn wistful time. Once, it said, we were a courageous bright young nation and now we are not. At the center of the celebration, there was a terrible dead quiet. In its aftermath, the country chose Jimmy Carter as its President—a man who said America must not expect too much of itself or of him, and wore blue jeans in the oval office.

In Aspen, hubris was not only alive and well—it was growing.

16 ^

Life Makes Fools
of All of Us

B USINESSMEN AND POLITICIANS had little left to
argue about. The mall, parks, trails and open meadows, the officially permissive attitude that received so
much press attention during the Claudine Longet trial,
the Aspen cops in factory-faded Levi's who cruised their
beats in smart little foreign cars had all become integral
parts of "the Aspen experience." Tourists liked them.
Businessmen advertised them. Commerce and nature
were united and business was better than ever.

But it was not supposed to have turned out this way.
The point had been to drive America out, not to draw it
in. Everything had been done right: bright, fearless liberals had been elected, zoning had been tightened to
slow development, open space had been preserved, cars
had been leashed. Yet something had gone wrong.

It was harder and harder to follow the leaders' reason-
ing. They seemed angry at the people, disappointed in
them. They spoke frequently of their own "sacrifices," of
sloth in their constituents. They didn't like questions,
challenges. It's lonely at the top, they implied, and we
know things that you don't know. They were Aspen's
new elite. They and their strongest supporters were the
best and the brightest of the new generation of Aspen

residents. Like all who had come before, they were highly educated, upper middle-class, confident and self-conscious. Unlike the Bayers, Benedicts and Gliddens, unlike Thompson and Vare, they were technicians: they believed that life—their own lives, the life of Aspen—could be adjusted, fine-tuned like a television set. They fine-tuned themselves with pills, weed, est, jogging; and they fine-tuned Aspen with ordinances, proscriptions, bans.

This new elite held most of the elected and appointed offices in both the city and the county. They led most of the crusades; worked at the radio stations and for Dunaway; ran Grass-Roots, the town's community TV station. Their training was generally in economics, law, math, planning—the more pragmatic subjects. They worshipped both nature and computers. In discussing a plan devised to block a state project supported by a majority of the people, one asserted that the people were basically stupid and didn't know what they wanted, so it was up to men like himself to make their decisions for them. Another one of them said, "There is nothing in the world to think about but yourself."

However uneasy the people of Aspen became, these now pols prevailed. If their original supporters grew bemused, disenchanted perhaps, new supporters from the business community replaced defections.

Their success was certified when a team led by Joe Edwards swept the 1976 county election and Stacy Standley was elected to a third term. Edwards, on surveying the crowds, the escalating real estate prices and the boutique boom, said that Aspen was on its way to becoming "a rich man's cliquey little dropout community." Having been in charge for four years, he was not admitting his own failure; rather, he was demonstrating the "I'm okay and you're not" objectivity that the new elitists, along with increasing numbers of citizens, practiced.

On the slate with Edwards were Richard "Dick Dove" Keinast and Michael Kinsley. Sheriff Carroll Whitmire had resigned, citing "pressures," following an investigation by the District Attorney's office. Edwards and Shellman appointed Keinast, who had run unsuccessfully against Whitmire in 1974, to replace him. Now Kienast was seeking voter approval of the appointment.

Kinsley was another Edwards-Shellman appointee. J. Sterling Baxter had decided not to seek re-election in 1974. There was no point: Shellman and Edwards had neutralized him. He chose Max Marolt, the fifties ski racer, to succeed him. Kinsley, who listed his occupation as "environmentalist," ran against Marolt. Marolt won, but soon thereafter suffered a mild heart attack and resigned. Colorado Governor Dick Lamm, on the advice of Edwards and Shellman, appointed Kinsley to replace Marolt. Thus democracy proceeded in Pitkin County. Liberals lost elections and won appointments, and conservatives were left out in the cold.

Shellman decided not to seek re-election. His seat was taken by Robert Child, a Republican rancher who had none of the usual biases of Pitkin County ranchers or Republicans. At the swearing-in, he read a poem he had written himself.

In 1976 gangs of conservatives entered the lists against Keinast and Kinsley. Among Keinast's opponents was Wilton "Wink" Jaffee, Jr., a successful New York stockbroker and Woody Creek rancher. Among Kinsley's opponents was Ramona Markalunas, a conservative who had beaten Vare in the city council race several years before. Keinast had degrees in philosophy and theology, had been, variously, a teacher, journalist, real estate man and cop. He believed in justice more than in either law or order. Kinsley described himself as "a Populist in Disneyland," and was as much in favor of the environment as he was against the Aspen Skiiing Corporation's ticket-pricing policies. They were both perfect Now Politicians. Edwards's opponent was former mayor Eve Homeyer. Standley's opponent was former mayor Barnard. Present and past toe to toe in the city and county. Another perfect test, residents said. The present won in a walk.

IT WAS THE LAST HURRAH for the conservatives. They didn't see that the game, 'he rules and the players had changed. Sheriff Keinast hung a sign on his wall that read, "To thine own self be true," and hired, for a time, a minister as jailer. The jailer ordered health-food platters for the prisoners, banned cigarettes, compelled exercise. One prisoner complained that the jailer's regimen constituted "cruel and unusual punishment." The jailer was unpenitent, saying he thought criminals might be "cured" by a proper diet, exercise and clean living.

Keinast decided that conventional lawmen would not make good deputies in Pitkin County, so he appointed a committee to interview "good people" for jobs in his department. Hunter Thompson was named to the committee, and a number of the applicants brought along poetry and short stories they'd written for Thompson to review. An observer at one committee meeting said, "They didn't want to be deputies, they wanted to be Hunter's protégés, for God's sake."

Mayor Standley dodged consistency in the way that skiers dodge rocks. He posed for a nude calendar, and was astonished when some of his constituents were shocked. He won office by promising to restrain growth, but later advocated that Aspen add "shoulders" to the summer season by soliciting spring and fall conventions. He blamed the town's "tarnished image" on the "bad attitudes" of the young workers who had been his first supporters.

Commissioner Shellman had been a leading opponent of growth. As a private citizen, he became Aspen's most aggressive spokesman for growth, tenaciously attacking the strict zoning ordinances and growth control measures he himself had written. The moment he was out of office, he could not resist having at the machinery he had created, going at it from a new angle, trying to take it apart or at least find its weaknesses.

In a town in constant motion, those who kept their ideals and ideas flexible were bound to prevail. By the late seventies Aspen seemed to be in perpetual motion, but unchanging, and increasingly prosperous. In 1960 retail sales in the county were $5 million. In 1970 they were $46 million. In 1978 they were $125 million, and both the county population and the number of tourist beds were double what they were in 1970. City and county budgets also both doubled. At the end of the seventies, in season, Aspen had the highest population density of any city or town in Colorado. In 1961 the assessed valuation of the county was $10.5 million. In 1972, when Shellman and Edwards took office, it was $56 million. In 1977 it was $128.5 million. The burghers sought their fortunes in the time-honored American way; the rebels sought truth and beauty in the time-honored American way; and together they made a profitable and pretty bonanza.

Not everything went up, of course. In 1969 there were 1.5 dwelling units per resident; in 1978 the ratio had declined to .77. Residents had begun moving down the valley to Basalt, Emma, Carbondale and various trailer parks. They were replaced by rich part-time residents who could, and apparently would, pay any price for a house in Aspen. Though per capita income rose slightly in the county between 1960 and 1972, it dropped .2 percent a year (with a correction for inflation) from 1976 to 1979. The average per capita income for 1979, when residents of independent means are not counted, was well below the national average. The cost of living in Aspen in 1979 was higher than in any other city in the continental United States.

The city-county Growth Management Plan approved in 1977 requires a 3.4 percent annual growth rate, or 319 units of housing spread across the county. This, on top of stringent zoning in both city and county, has created a housing crunch in Aspen that is as bad or worse than any housing shortage in the country and has driven real estate prices up and up. A house that might sell for $20,000 in Denver sold for $325,000 in Aspen in the fall of 1979. Modest condominiums that sold for $100,000 in 1977 sold for over $200,000. Four hundred dollars a month for a studio apartment was considered a bargain.

The city and county, having created the crunch, tried to ease it. Inducements were offered to developers to build "moderate cost" housing. Since 1978, every new development must contain some "permanent moderate cost" housing. The county itself built a moderately priced condominium complex; the city has one in the works. But at the moment no one with less than $150,-000 to buy, or $1,000 a month to rent, can live well in Aspen. In January 1979 Edwards told a developer who requested a relaxation of zoning regulations in order to build some inexpensive houses that keeping the valley open was the commission's first priority. So the locals have become commuters.

The housing shortage led to an employee shortage. In the winter of 1978 workers were so hard to find that one condominium complex offered maids $7 an hour and a free trip to Mexico at the end of the season. The pols and the businessmen didn't demonstrate much sympathy. Standley worried that "the tourist experience is going to start slipping downhill." A lodge owner complained, "It's a manager's nightmare—they've got the upper hand," ignoring the housing nightmare that "they" faced. Neither pols nor businessmen expressed any concern over the loss of residents. In late 1978 lodges and condominiums began importing Vietnamese refugees to do the menial jobs. It was said that they came cheap and expected little.

Some long-time residents, professional people and small businessmen, finding life in Aspen too rich for them, began to move out too. Santa Fe, New Mexico, Santa Barbara, California, and San Francisco all have growing contingents of Aspen exiles. In describing the search for a new home town, one person declared, "I'm going to find someplace really ugly. No trees, no water, nothing but rocks, a place that no one could possibly like."

IF THE PEOPLE were disenchanted with their leadership, the leaders seemed to be growing increasingly impatient with the people. In the early seventies the businessmen thought to improve the people. The Aspen Chamber of Commerce created a "smile committee," which laid out an eleven-step program: "1. a small nucleus of employers initiate the program by insisting on good, smiling, courteous service; 2. at least two employer-employee meetings (perhaps just prior to each season) to explain what we as a community must do to maintain our number-one status; what we, as employers, expect of our employees; how they might earn larger tips; a history of the community; a monetary monthly reward for each business's most outstanding employee; 3. a lodge-of-the-month program; 4. a rebate to employees who have worked a certain period of time and who have complied with our requirements; in the form of discounted lift tickets, food, clothing, gasoline, etc.; 5. an A, B, C decal or sticker to be posted on the entrance of every restaurant, designating general cleanliness and sanitation levels, as determined by monthly, unscheduled inspections; 6. fire everyone using the word "turkey;" 7. eliminate the word "local;" 8. if we, as employers, can have an employee-of-the-month, why can't the town sponsor a guest-of-the-week program, selected by the mayor and the president of the chamber of commerce spontaneously off the street, then put his picture in the paper, give him a free meal, one night's lodging; 9. have everybody wear a smile button with their name on it, so guests are immediately on a first-name basis with us; 10. request that the broadcasting companies begin short ('gee, we're glad you decided to ski Aspen today') blurb, perhaps four times a day; 11. find out how far and in which ways the press might participate with us."

The Smile Committee was laughed out of existence by the people, but in the summer of 1978, the self-styled maverick mayor, Stacy Standley, perhaps unwittingly echoed its theme in a stern lecture to the Chamber of Commerce. The onetime bartender said, in part, "Our lodging is not up to the standards of the industry . . . the attitudes of shop owners and employees are almost hostile." Calling for some sort of lodge rating system, he

said, "The ski corp with its package ski plans could exclude all lodges which do not live up to the rating system.
Only lodges that submitted to the lodge rating and up-
graded according to the rating system could participate
in the ski program. There should be something like that
for the restaurants and shops, too."

Though a survey showed that most residents were unwilling to walk more than 1,000 feet away from their cars
and a plan to double the size of the mall was defeated by
voters in the spring of 1979, the Now Politicians have
continued their effort to reduce the number of cars in
city and county through the creation of what they call
"auto disincentives." The mall, a ban on car rental agencies at the airport, city and county bus lines and a proposed "busway" that will exclude cars are all part of the
effort.

Perhaps the most hotly debated disincentive is the
official reluctance to cooperate with the Colorado State
Highway Department's plan to improve State Highway
82, the only road into Aspen. Referred to by locals as
"Killer 82," the two-lane highway is in chronically poor
repair and, in season, is clogged with cars. The Highway-
men have proposed adding two additional lanes and
changing the route to eliminate some of its more treacherous curves. Local officials have steadfastly opposed
both the four-laning and the route change, saying that
shoring up shoulders and adding turn lanes at busy inter-
sections would be sufficient. The number of accidents on
the highway demonstrates its dangers, but the Now
Politicians claim that enlarging it will merely increase
the number of cars using it and therefore increase the
number of accidents. After pushing for a wider road for
a number of years, the state backed off, which caused a

number of residents to go over local officials' heads to the governor.

A petition claimed that a majority of Pitkin County residents wanted the road improved. Many local cars sported bumper stickers demanding a new highway. Regular straw votes showed a majority of citizens favor four-laning. In 1979 the Highway Department did make some crucial repairs, but as one resident said, "They won't really fix the road until those commissioners go to them on bended knee, and they aren't about to do that."

Both city and county officials claim that the upper end of the valley is threatened by a chronic traffic jam and a killer smog. They have already invested in expensive smog-measuring devices. In season, there are lots of cars in town, and auto exhaust does get trapped over Aspen. But the measuring equipment only works occasionally, and no concrete evidence exists to show that the officials' doomsaying is justified. When they discussed the possibility of banning fireplaces because wood smoke was a pollutant, virtually everyone protested.

In other efforts to safeguard the health of their constituents, the county commissioners have banned candy and cigarette machines and a bar from the new airport terminal, and soft drink machines from the courthouse. City and county leaders collaborated on a law to ban smoking in many public places. Outlaw smokers in either city or county can get a $300 fine and ninety days in jail for smoking in the wrong places, and as one angry resident noted, "You have to know what the wrong places are."

But if caffeine, sugar and nicotine were out, marijuana, hashish and cocaine seemed to be in. In 1977 a federal official called Aspen "the cocaine capital of America;" *People* magazine reported that cocaine was as easy to find in Aspen as the more conventional snow. Denver TV stations and newspapers regularly report on "the wide-open drug scene" in Aspen. Through most of the seventies, city and county law enforcement agencies were unwilling to cooperate with any undercover state or federal drug investigations in Aspen; and after a wave of protests from residents, they curtailed their own undercover investigations. The sheriff and the Aspen Police Department have stated that private drug users are not likely to be prosecuted in the county as long as they are discreet. This policy, they say, reflects "community attitudes" toward drugs. But in 1979, after a Denver TV station did a series of reports on the "drug scene" in Aspen alleging that anyone could get any sort of drug easily and that many people did, the Aspen Valley Improvement Association issued a statement saying that drug use was epidemic in Aspen and not condoned by many residents.

The AVIA, an alliance of prosperous residents and part-time residents, claimed to have evidence of rampant drug abuse and lax law enforcement that verged on collusion with dope dealers, but it would not say where its evidence came from. At the same time, the AVIA called for an investigation of the drug scene in Aspen and a public denunciation by residents of official policy, promising to cooperate with any "responsible" effort to put the lid on drug use in Aspen. Late in 1979 a federal grand jury was convened in Denver and subpoenas were issued to a number of Aspen residents. Purportedly the grand jury was examining the role of Aspen and Pitkin County law enforcement agencies in short-circuiting a massive federal drug raid in the valley in the summer of 1979. Some federal agents were said to have alleged that while they had caught a few small dealers, the big ones escaped. Apparently, nothing came of the grand jury proceedings. In the spring of 1980, during a segment of the CBS-TV show *60 Minutes*, an FBI agent and a DEA agent reiterated their dissatisfaction with Pitkin county law officers, and Keinast reiterated his belief in the primacy of individual rights as stated in the U.S. Constitution. Subsequently, *60 Minutes* reported that the majority of their mail about the segment had praised Keinast's views. Such viewer unanimity was unprecedented, according to CBS.

Some residents insist that even though drugs are available in Aspen, it is not a serious problem. Others insist that drug use is a major problem and that the sheriff and police have been derelict. The lawmen are, at the moment, silent on the subject.

In a much-discussed 1979 case, a security guard at Starwood, the most expensive and exclusive subdivision in the valley, was convicted of supplying drugs to children of some of the valley's leading citizens. His conviction triggered a flood of letters to the *Aspen Times.* About half the writers seemed to feel the guard was a scapegoat; others said he deserved what he got. A few said it was a lot of noise over nothing.

AMERICA NO LONGER seemed even interesting in the late 1970s. Elvis Presley died. Jimmy Carter pardoned draft evaders. There seemed to be more terrible plane wrecks, more hurricanes, more earthquakes than there had ever been before. Women claimed they were making some gains; blacks said they weren't. The debate over the morality and legality of abortion went on. Smokey the Bear died. Oil prices continued to rise, as did unemployment, and the value of the dollar was still declining. The government charged big American companies had paid bribes to foreign governments to win favors, and the news media revealed that congressmen had taken bribes from South Korea.

Movies like *One Flew over the Cuckoo's Nest, Nashville, Network* and *All the President's Men* tried to plumb the American malaise, but *Rocky, Saturday Night Fever* and *Star Wars* were bigger box office hits. In another New York blackout, 3,700 people were arrested during a wave of looting and vandalism. Nine hundred and seventeen members of the People's Temple, a California-born religious group that moved to Jonestown, Guyana, killed themselves or were murdered on orders of their leader Jim Jones. Norman Rockwell died. President Carter said the nation was suffering "a crisis of confidence." Someone in Aspen named it the United States of Disco. But disco was in Aspen. Everything was in Aspen.

Accused mass-murderer Ted Bundy was in the Pitkin County jail. He had been extradicted from Utah to face murder charges in Aspen. During a preliminary hearing, he leapt out of a second-floor courtroom window and vanished. For nearly a week he eluded county and state cops as he roamed around the mountains. He was caught weaving down the road in a stolen car by deputies who initially thought he was just another drunk driver. Sheriff Keinast transferred Bundy to the Garfield County jail for safekeeping, rejected suggestions that he resign, but accepted the resignations of three deputies and fired a secretary, saying that the employee exodus was not triggered by Bundy's escape, but resulted from "disagreement with my philosophy of law enforcement." On New Year's Eve Bundy escaped through a light fixture in the ceiling of his cell. He was located many weeks later in Florida, where he was charged with and subsequently convicted of multiple murders. Aspen's District Attorney Frank Tucker flew to Florida, vowing to bring Bundy back to Colorado to stand trial. Shortly thereafter, Tucker himself was on trial for embezzling funds, some of which he was charged with using to pay for a young girl's abortion. Tucker claimed she was a valued "drug informant," but he lost his job anyway and wound up doing time in jail himself.

When he was stopped on suspicion of "driving under the influence," former county commissioner Dwight Shellman locked his car doors, perhaps planning to stay inside his car until he felt better, but the cop finally talked him into surrendering. Shellman then arranged to have his trail moved to Glenwood Springs, claiming that he could not get a fair hearing in Pitkin County Judge John Wendt's courtroom. Former D.A. Wendt had begun giving virtually automatic thirty-day jail sentences to anyone convicted of drunk driving. Townspeople called him "the Hanging Judge," but were also less inclined to drive when they'd had too much to drink. Shellman claimed Wendt had hated him for years. He went around Aspen locating people who could testify that they'd heard Wendt express negative opinions of him. Many people who had been at the Jerome bar, where Shellman had been drinking prior to his arrest, offered to testify for the prosecution. But in the end, Shellman managed to get a change of venue to Glenwood Springs where he was found guilty of a lesser charge, reckless driving, and fined $100.

It became harder and harder to tell the good guys from the bad guys.

17 ⌃
The Pleasure of Business

T HERE IS an old saying that one must be very careful
what one wishes for, because one will get it. Aspen
wanted everything and got it, and then wanted more
because everything turned out to be not enough.

For a while, there was an appealing innocence about
its appetite, a certain grace. It was like the child on
Christmas Day who wants all the presents under the tree
for himself. I'll have the mountains, it said, and all the
snow, and summer concerts and blue skies and just
enough people from other places to support these
things. They will be very nice polite people who will
come and go on schedule, so that spring and fall will be
very peaceful. They will admire the beauty of the place
and the integrity of the people and the happy life that
is lived here, but they will not overstay their welcome.

Later its appetite grew, multiplied, got clumsier. The
town became something like the teen-ager who wants to
eat the candy, but not get the pimples or gain the weight
that inevitably follow. It still wanted the beauty and the
serenity of the place, but wanted, too, a certain prosperity. It is an enormous valley, after all. There is probably
room here for more people than we once thought. With
a little prosperity and more people, we can have more

ski runs and more concerts and more of the finer things for ourselves. Ski posters and hot dogs are all right, but Oldenburg sketches and lamb chops are more suitable to our higher station. It will be all right. We can handle it because we have no billboards, no ghettos and no fast-food parlors. Many people have become prosperous, after all, and not been corrupted by it; and we are strong and happy people, and therefore impervious to corruption.

Still later it grew bored with the same old truth, beauty and prosperity. Its tastes had got more sophisticated. "The mountains are beautiful, the town is pleasant enough, it is good to be strong and happy, but it would be better to be powerful and original. We will control the place and free the people, improve the town and the weather, and liberate the citizenry to find such pleasures as it wishes." It was a little like the lady who redecorates her house annually and gives parties with "themes" because ordinary parties are passé.

By the late seventies, Aspen's appetite had become an addiction—desperate, even crude. The town was like the drunk who lies to everyone including himself, plays tricks on himself and others, insists on his innocence, says, "I am not a drunk," blinking, avoiding your eyes. In the same way, Aspen said, "I am not greedy," and avoided looking at itself.

Having vigorously opposed new ski areas throughout the seventies because every enlargement of the ski terrain triggered an expansion of the town, in 1978 residents approved plans for a new ski area, Little Annie, east of Aspen Mountain. Developer David Farny said it would be "a locals' area" which would serve to restore the flagging sense of community, and would therefore not set off another round of growth. A majority of resi-

dents chose to believe him. The proposed area included some of the best ski terrain in the Rockies, and Farny had promised to keep lift rates low.

Though county officials opposed Little Annie because it would violate the Growth Management Plan in both tangible and intangible ways, such community leaders as architect Fritz Benedict, *Times* publisher Bil Dunaway and singer and self-styled environmentalist John Denver supported Farny publically and invested in Little Annie. They argued that it was a potentially superb ski area and would offer much-needed competition to the Aspen Skiing Corporation. Dunaway further argued that his financial interest in Little Annie and his editorial support for it did not imply collusion, but was merely common sense. He was praised in certain quarters for his logic as well as his candor.

Everyone knew the area would inevitably cause more growth, but there were acres of deep powder on Little Annie. They would worry about growth later. Aspen's devotion to pleasure, the post-puritan ethic, the liberated mind in the limber body, its elevation of ME over THEM and US and YOU were finally paramount. Pleasure is expensive, but it is also profitable. The pleasures of the place were sold to pay for the pleasures of the people.

Business became the main thing. Politics was a sideline again. In an important Home Rule Charter vote in the county, only 7 percent of the registered voters cast ballots, and showed their disenchantment with the status quo by voting to enlarge the Pitkin County Commission to five members. If you can't beat them, dilute them. The incumbents' opposition to such instruments of pleasure as Little Annie, a bar and cars at the airport and Coca-Cola in the courthouse had clearly outraged the

voters. In the 1978 county election, incumbents Michael Kinsley and Richard Keinast were challenged by city councilman George Parry and former state highway patrolman Roy Griffith, respectively. Kinsley played the man of the people, Parry the friend of the tourist. Keinast promised to continue his unorthodox approach to law and order. Griffith promised a return to traditional law enforcement. No one was listening. When it was done, the incumbents were re-elected.

People who had once joked about their burgeoning business and the ridiculous real estate prices weren't joking anymore. If annual grosses did not increase by 20 percent, emergency meetings with accountants were scheduled. Storekeepers who once chose merchandise because they liked it began looking for sure-fire sales items. A bookstore that once had eschewed such nonbooks as self-help manuals now displayed what seemed to be acres of them. At one time, anything that looked like an Aspen souvenir was rejected by shopkeepers, but now one could make a life out of the souvenir stuff, which ranged from post cards to clothes. Tee-shirt merchants not only produced endless variations on the Aspen theme, but commemorated every event with a new tee shirt. Six hours after Ted Bundy leapt from the courthouse window, people were wearing Bundy tee shirts. The *Aspen Times* grew fatter and fatter. In some weeks of winter, the country weekly ran over a hundred pages and bore more resemblance to a catalogue than a newspaper.

At the close of the 1970s, small condominiums rented for upward of $400 a day in high season in winter. Some houses went for over $1,000 a day, causing increasing numbers of Aspen families to leave home for Christmas so they could rent their houses. The West End's charming Victorian houses, refurbished by owners who bought them in the fifties for perhaps $20,000, were worth close to half a million dollars on the Aspen market. The unexpected bonanza created a dilemma for the owners of these houses. Some sold; more talked of selling. They had not only found the pot of gold, they were literally sitting in it, and it was not comfortable. Should they take the money and run? Should they sell and buy something else, something cheaper? There wasn't much that *was* cheaper or as pleasant. Should they condominiumize? Could they condominiumize? The questions seemed to be moral as well as legal and financial. They were put to psychiatrists as well as accountants. One resident told her new accountant that she looked on him as her priest and shrink as well as her financial advisor. He nodded, suggesting that she was not the first client to see him in that light.

In 1979 there were fifty real estate firms in Aspen, with hundreds of people possessing or applying for broker's licenses. It was possible to imagine a day when everyone would have real estate broker's licenses along with driver's licenses and Social Security cards. People talked about real estate—sales, buys, prices, possibilities —almost obsessively. A stranger arriving in Aspen knowing nothing about it would surely believe that the town was, first of all, a giant real estate firm.

A couple of years before, Carbondale citizens complained that Aspen real estate speculators were trying to take over their town, noting that an Aspen woman had bought an old building and immediately tripled tenants' rents. Aspen people also made speculative real estate investments in Glenwood Springs, Rifle (where the oil shale is) and other mountain towns. Housewives, ski patrolmen, almost everyone wanted to play real estate for fun and profit, and almost everyone was defensive about it. Only ten years ago these same people had been calling speculators "greedheads" and "land rapers." Aspen was full of Fausts. That was how they saw themselves, as selling out to the Devil.

It was not that they minded the money. As it turned out, Aspen people were just as ambitious, just as interested in money as everyone else. Though they came to it late, they made money as avidly and as well as old hands. But since they did not like being thought ordinary, their prosperity was attended by drama, agony, embarrassment.

Whether money accumulated through hard work or good luck, no one was willing to speak candidly of his or her fortune. No one said, "I bought this house for 20 thou and I can sell it for 500 thou. God damn, what a lucky break!" They spoke instead of the responsibilities, the options, the terrible choices. Bil Dunaway enjoyed talking about his media accomplishments, but got red in the face and stuttered when his real estate ventures were mentioned. Shopkeepers, dedicated pros who had invested years of work, dissembled, laughed, said, "God, one minute I had three Norwegian sweaters and four pairs of ski boots and the next thing I knew I had . . . made . . . all . . . this . . . money." One got the impression that all of Aspen's new rich would be happier to admit they'd robbed a bank than made . . . money . . . in . . . business . . . or . . . real . . . estate.

But if there was embarrassment in the making of money, there was ample solace in the spending of it. Each year hundreds of thousands of tourists paid a lot of dough to ski or go to concerts and lectures in Aspen. Each year Aspen residents went off at the height of the winter season to ski the Bugaboos in Canada or the deep powder in Alta. They went to Arizona for marathon tennis, to Hawaii for surfing, to the South Pacific for sailing. Many Aspen residents purchased private planes, some of them jets. Others owned hot air balloons, one of which costs several thousand dollars to launch. When in residence in the late seventies, they rode to the hounds on thoroughbred horses, played tennis, darted over to Lake Powell for a weekend or down to the Golden Door for a workout. They took courses in wine-tasting, or played polo, or shopped along with the tourists. They ate and drank very well. They jogged in the morning. They regularly had their backs massaged, their horoscopes done "professionally," their hair "styled." They bought paintings and sculptures and commissioned stained-glass windows and went into the mountains in "customized" jeeps. Their children were sent off to the best boarding schools, sported the gear of Olympic champions on the slopes, had cars and stereo sets and TV sets of their own, as well as guitars and videotape recorders.

The conversation over roast beef and Château Margaux at dinner parties turned to the good old days. In "the good old days," they were penniless, they were outrageous, and they were happy. They didn't worry about money in the good old days because they had no money. Now they had money and they worried about it —the making of it, the spending of it, the saving of it, the meaning of it. They asked unanswerable questions. Did we ruin Aspen? Did it ruin us? Is it all over? Is the bubble going to burst again?

There were exceptions, of course. People who stood out of the way of the commotion, who just got on with their work or who managed to miss the boat, whose pleasures remained simple. A certain tension came to exist between the two groups. One of the old poor said

to one of the new rich, "God, I'm really tired of having to move every year. It'd be nice to find a place I could stay for two or three years without having the landlord announce he has to raise the rent or condominiumize or go short-term or some damn thing." The new rich representative said, "It's your own damn fault. You should have bought something when you came. You could have bought any house in town for $10,000 then." The old poor representative said, "I didn't have $10,000 twenty years ago, for God's sake." The new rich representative said, "Well, that's not my fault."

In the fifties the business of America was business and the business of Aspen was happiness. In the sixties in Aspen it was seen that happiness and business were not necessarily at odds. In the seventies happiness was defined as pleasure and pleasure was defined as MORE. More is, of course, the first principle of business.

FROM 1977 TO 1979, downtown Aspen nearly doubled in size. A new commercial center spilled across Main Street, beyond the Hotel Jerome, all the way to the Roaring Fork River. The city's new electric station, a savings and loan building, a building that houses the *Aspen Times* printing plant and about ten other stores and businesses, and a behemoth of a building that houses a grocery store, numerous other stores and some apartments were all in place. A new post office, other stores and businesses and, if Fritz Benedict has his way, a mix of townhouses, shops, restaurants, a parking structure and a large performing arts center will be added. West of this new commercial district is the Aspen Center for Environmental Studies at Hallam Lake, one of the few wild game preserves inside an American city. It was created by and is in large part sustained by Elizabeth Paepcke.

She wants to buy up the land between the stores and the lake to create a buffer between the animals and the people, but escalating prices jeopardize the plan. Directly to the east of the new buildings, but across the river, is Aspen's new Visual Arts Center, which opened in June 1979 with a show of works by such masters as Willem De Kooning, Andy Warhol and Robert Rauschenberg. A collaborative effort of the city, the county and the citizenry, it is an old building smartly refurbished.

In December 1977, Twentieth Century Fox Film Corporation offered $48.6 million for all of the Aspen Skiing Corporation stock, or $45 a share for stock that was selling over the counter for $17. As one Skiing Corporation director put it, "It was too good an offer to refuse." The sale was completed in June 1978. With its vast Aspen holdings, the ski area at Breckenridge, Colorado, Fortress Mountain near Banff, Canada, and its investment in Bacquiera-Beret, Spain, the Aspen Skiing Corporation is probably the largest and most successful ski area operator in the world, for all its bad reputation in Aspen. Dennis Stanfill, chairman of the board of Fox, said at the time of the offer that the 17 percent annual compound growth rate of the Skiing Corporation in the 1970s was its primary appeal. After the purchase was completed, Stanfill came to Aspen and told a Chamber of Commerce meeting that Fox would be "a good corporate citizen" in Aspen.

Snowmass Resort changed hands about the same time that the Skiing Corporation became "Fox Country." Permanent residents voted to incorporate as Snowmass Village and elected a mayor and other officials. A limited partnership, the Snowmass Land Company, bought the assets of the Snowmass Corporation from American Cement for $7 million. The assets include 2,900 acres of undeveloped land, the Snowmass Real Estate Company, an eighteen-hole golf course, a bar, a restaurant and a ranch that specializes in rodeos.

Two of the principals in the Snowmass Land Company are former officers of the Sea Pines Company, developer of another posh enclave, Hilton Head Island, South Carolina. Immediate plans included development of the land. Under guidelines previously worked out with the county commissioners, as many as 2,500 new houses and condominiums could be built. One of the new owners said, "We are studying the feasability of creating a club which will serve skiers as well as golfers and tennis players." In 1979 there were accommodations for 6,000 people and 14 restaurants and shops at Snowmass Resort. Baldy is the second largest ski mountain in America, with 11 lifts, 1,350 acres of bowls and trails and the capability of accommodating 11,000 skiers. It is the most profitable of the Skiing Corporation's three mountains in Aspen.

The Aspen Institute's ties to Aspen became, in the late 1970s, increasingly tenuous and the relationship between the two has also become increasingly fractious. The Institute's main offices were moved to New York, and it established offices and programs in several other American cities, as well as Berlin, Germany. In 1978 it was given the Wye Plantation, a huge and historic estate in Maryland. At the same time that Institute chairman Anderson was claiming, "We still consider Aspen our home," an Institute vice-president said Wye is "the place we call home." A large piece of the Institute campus was subdivided and sold in 1977; it was soon studded with large houses. In the summer of 1979, Institute officials announced it had a new Colorado campus, and that some of its Aspen programs would be moved to the new site.

Located in the San Luis Valley in southeastern Colorado, the new campus is part of a 100,000-acre ranch owned by AZL, Inc. AZL's chairman is Maurice Strong, a founding director of the U.N. Environmental Program as well as an Institute trustee. Strong donated 300 acres of his Baca Grande development to the Institute, along with an inn, golf course, stables, swimming pool, tennis courts and a number of houses. The addition of seminar rooms was planned. The nearest town is Crestone; the nearest town of any size, Alamosa, a typical Colorado small town, is forty miles away from Baca Grande.

An Institute press release quoted Strong as saying that the Institute's imminent arrival was "an exciting development in his company's plans to develop Baca Grande as an intellectual, cultural and conservation center." In the same press release, Anderson was quoted as saying, "There is merit in also having available for programs the more simple, austere and less costly environment that the Aspen Institute once enjoyed. It is a special opportunity that is beyond the reach of our present facilities in Aspen."

Institute president Joseph Slater said that Aspen had changed from a sleepy mountain community to an expensive resort and contrasted the spacious, rustic "pioneering" ambience of the San Luis Valley with the hustle and bustle of Aspen. "Baca has this marvelous sense of space, openness, with trails. It is more conducive to reflection and has space for private discussions, reflections and walks."

Anderson's disenchantment with Aspen's increasingly hectic pace was nothing new. Two years before, in an interview with *Aspen* magazine, he said, "Trying to run something of a serious nature in a town that is dedicated

only to fun is probably one of our permanent problems.
. . . Imagine trying to run a great university in Las
Vegas."

As chairman of the board of the Atlantic-Richfield Corporation (ARCO), Anderson has pumped a great deal of
money into the Institute. It has been the regular recipi-
ent of corporation and foundation grants, but it continues to lose money. In 1976 officials announced plans to
build a large hotel on the Institute campus. They needed
the additional facilities, they said, and they needed the
money the hotel would bring in. It would make the Institute finally self-supporting. The city council and the
Planning and Zoning Commission refused to approve
the plan on the grounds that such a hotel would alter the
character of Aspen's West End and would violate the
Growth Management Plan. The Institute scaled down its
ambitious plans, but it refused to give the city concrete
assurances that it would remain headquartered in Aspen
and that the hotel would not be turned into just another
tourist circus.

At one point, the Institute entered into negotiations to
sell its Aspen facilities to the University of Colorado, but
members of the state legislature objected to a public
university investing money in an elitist think-tank. Later
Anderson entered into an agreement with the University of Denver to share facilities and combine programs.
The plan came to nothing. Institute officials accused the
young pols of being philistines with no conception of the
Institute's international prominence. The young pols
countered by saying that the Institute had become just
another developer trying to cash in on Aspen's success.
In the fall of 1979, simultaneous with its announcement
of the new Baca Grande campus, the Institute sued the
city, claiming that its rights were being violated by the

arbitrary refusal of the city to permit the expansion.

Residents' attitudes were mixed. Some agreed with the city council, others with the Institute. Some feared the economic impact of the loss of the Institute as a major summer attraction. Others claimed that the Institute was a joke, noting that from time to time it has been harshly criticized in the media.

Several years ago in *(MORE)*, a now defunct journalism review, author Peter Schrag denounced the Institute Program on Communications and Society as a kind of high-toned hustle. It had received over a million dollars in foundation money and had produced nothing but "studies of studies," he said. When ARCO bought the London *Observer, Village Voice* columnist Alexander Cockburn lambasted Anderson, his chief minions Joseph Slater and Douglas Cater (a one-time White House aide, writer, and Anderson's media man) and the Institute. He wrote, in part, "This think-tank in the Rockies . . . has long been a crossroads of corporate-intellectual comity and mutual reassurance . . . [It] has sessions in which the CIA intellectuals and right-center intellectual bureaucrats are only too delighted to enjoy free bed and board, caper along mountain trails and give seminars to business executives on the meaning of Plato in the modern boardroom and the 'interface' (a big Aspen word) between education and communications. . . . Aspen has become a center of intellectual boondogglers and corporate patrons. . . ."

When asked about the Institute's much-bruited "thought leading to action" programs, an administrator at a large American university said, "Little thought, no action at all, but one enjoys being in Aspen."

Herbert Bayer had led the effort to pass the 1955 zoning ordinance. The Master Plan was his idea and was partially paid for by the Institute. The Growth Management Plan grew out of the Master Plan. In 1979, while Aspen was not the most aesthetically pure town in America, it was certainly the most aesthetically self-conscious—tuning its controls, agonizing over every addition to the townscape, passing official judgments on everything from business signs to house plans, anxiously cataloguing previous mistakes and vowing not to repeat them. All of that began with Bayer, bore his mark. But Bayer was as outraged as Anderson by the city's stand.

In Paepcke's time, the goals of the Institute and Aspen were synonymous. The mutual discontent was a measure of the grip business had on Aspen in the seventies. According to Slater, the goal of the Institute was nothing less than playing a central role in the shaping of international policy. Summer seminars focused on Middle Eastern problems (though one Israeli group claimed in 1979 that the "problems" are inevitably Arab problems). The wife of the former Shah of Iran was at the end of 1979 an honorary trustee of the Institute. Former Secretary of State Henry Kissinger was an Institute fellow and a frequent Aspen visitor. There is a great deal of oil in the Middle East. ARCO is a leading oil company. The last time the Shah's wife was in Aspen, Iranian students staged a protest. One placard said, "The Shah is not a humanist." If hedonists had overcome humanists in Aspen, business seemed to have overtaken the humanists at the Institute.

The Aspen Music Festival and School looked more and more like big business too. Edgar Stern, a Sears Roebuck heir and a kind of individual conglomerate with business interests in New Orleans, Park City, Utah and San Francisco, succeeded Courtlandt D. Barnes, Jr., as chairman of the board of the Music Associates of Aspen in 1974.

Under Stern's leadership, both the Festival and School grew, and were it not for the upward spiral of housing costs for its 900 music students, it might actually have broken even.

The continuing deficit bothered Stern and his fellow trustees; in 1979 they began talking about moving the Festival to Snowmass Resort, where housing was available at reasonable rates. Like Anderson, Stern said that the increasingly hectic Aspen townscape was not compatible with the Festival and School. Nevertheless he supported Anderson's proposed hotel, even though it would be adjacent to the tent and presumably less than pastoral.

Aspen residents have always seen the Festival as the town's crowning cultural achievement and as an integral part of Aspen, as much a part of it as the mountains. Its removal would not only be a blow to the town's economy, it would diminish the place itself. The music and musicians are as vital to Aspen as fish and plant life are to a stream. It is that fundamental, residents said. Many of them supported the Festival with generous annual contributions and regular attendance at concerts; but some of these same residents continued to raise rental fees on the houses, lodges and condominiums that housed music students and musicians in the summer, claiming the escalating rents were necessary to offset their own rising costs.

Anderson likened Aspen to Las Vegas and wanted to build the biggest hotel of all. Stern claimed rents had risen too high in Aspen, possibly necessitating removal of the Festival. Residents wept, but did not lower the rents. The music is vital, they cried. But so is real estate. Business, pleasure, art, sport, Aspen: they became synonymous.

IN 1980 EVERYONE is having his way in Aspen and getting everything he wants, and that is the American way. America has returned the favor by making Aspen an American capital, but residents remain unsatisfied and self-conscious. They have done nothing wrong, but they must have done something wrong. It was not meant to turn out this way. Aspen was not supposed to become an American capital. It was supposed to stay out there on the edge, ahead, behind, off to the side, but surely not in step, surely not that. They did nothing right, but they must have done something right. What was it? How did it go right?

They know that there are people out there in America who dream of Aspen. Young people, kids really, who think Aspen is where it's happening. They know that there is an Aspen mystique, because when they go other places and say that they are from Aspen, people say, "Oh God, Aspen. It must be wonderful in Aspen. I'm going to Aspen someday." They smile and nod and wonder what those people will think when they actually see Aspen. These are not people who will be touched by boutiques and disco blare and Kissinger, for God's sake. These are young, eager kids who will expect . . . MORE somehow.

IT WAS LATE one night toward the end of the summer of 1979. The Festival was over. The tent was being taken down. The canvas hung in great sheets over the wire struts. Paepcke Auditorium, beyond the tent, was absolutely still. Cones of light marked it like a temple. The seminarians were gone.

In one of the houses in the new Institute subdivision, people in tennis clothes were gathered around a bar, drinking, laughing. In another house, disco lights were flashing on and off, and I could hear a disco version of "Let the Sunshine In," a hit song from *Hair*. On Red Mountain, directly above this disco house, another house was ablaze with lights. It looked like a night club or a restaurant glowing there on the side of the shaggy mountain. It belonged to Frank Butler, the brother of the producer of *Hair* and a leading Aspen party-giver. It was said that the lights went on automatically every night, whether Butler was giving a party or not. The house was named "Starship."

This was perhaps not what Ortega had in mind, but it was surely "a total synthesis of life."

18 ⌃
Phantom Battles in
a Real Landscape

A MERICA, the first and last wonderland, is more than the sum of its parts. It is a concept, a fantasy, a dream. It is simultaneously itself and the idea of itself, and the idea is still more compelling than the reality. America is not perfect. The idea of America is perfect.

Aspen is more than the sum of its parts, is an idea too. In 1974 the Aspen Institute commissioned Sidney Hyman, an associate professor of Criminal Justice at the University of Illinois, to write an account of the Institute's founding, development and accomplishments. The book was called *The Aspen Idea.* From time to time, the Aspen idea was discussed in town meetings, though not recently. In 1980 people speak less of the idea of Aspen, more of "the Aspen way of life" or "the Aspen experience." Aspen was a place, became and idea, now it is also an adjective. Walter Paepcke spoke of "freedom and responsibility," of endlessly challenging mind and body, of the self-discipline that begets greatness, but he didn't talk much about "the Aspen idea." Hyman suggested that "the Aspen idea" was to approach everything from a humanistic perspective. In 1980 people often talk of Aspen when they talk about "liberation." Liberation as expressed in the Aspen way of life and the

Aspen experience doesn't seem to have a lot to do with freedom and responsibility, but a connection can be seen. Evolution occurs regardless of any value we may put on it, and the evolution from Paepcke's notion of "freedom and responsibility" to "liberation" was probably inevitable.

Omaha describes nothing but Omaha. Atlanta describes nothing but Atlanta. But America describes more than America and Aspen describes more than Aspen; and here and now each to some extent describes the other. America and Aspen seemed to be opposites for thirty years, but opposites attract in powerful ways. Aspen the place is in love with America the idea, as America the place is in love with Aspen the idea. The *idea* of America has much more to do with liberation than the *fact* of America.

Aspen loves the idea of America as endless, limitless, promising. It loves the possibility of imminent perfection and complete freedom, loves the idea that fame and fortune and beauty and truth are available to believers, and Aspen believes. America itself is like the boy who had to drop out of high school and go to work too soon. It lost its youth first, and then its innocence, and it has been looking for that lost innocence for a very long time. It went west, roamed across the plains and deserts and mountains, and found only more hard work. When it ran out of land, it wheeled and went into the cities. There it found not innocence, but many other rewards, rich but insufficient. Still on the lookout, it prowled the land again, and came across Aspen. Aspen had all the characteristics of innocence. It was small, remote, out of time, out of step, young, carefree, fresh, naive, chaste. Hubris and innocence are almost synonymous. Aspen had always seen itself as innocent, and for all its mixed feelings about America, it was touched by its recognition, determined to live up to the accolade.

Hubris shows up in Aspen in every public forum, in conversation, in attitudes and actions. A man paints an enormous rude finger on the roof of his barn. Joggers pass in the road and do not acknowledge one another. These people want what everyone wants: everything. The valley, the mountains, the whole damn continent.

Stalled somewhere between the frontier and civilization, Aspen offers a somber nation the unexamined but perfect life. In Aspen, the last citadel of innocence, credit and blame are assigned to full moons, plummeting barometers, the stars, eccentric clovers, esoteric exercises, biorhythms, gurus, abstinence, fasting, wellness, whatever gets you through the night. I'm okay . . . and you're not.

TM, est, martial arts, Zen, arica, Jehovah's Witnesses, Trout Unlimited, the Environmental Task Force, the Sierra Club, Common Cause, the Rotary Club, Lions, Elks, Eagles, bridge, backgammon, volleyball, soccer, rugby, softball, kayaking, skiing, jogging, climbing, hang-gliding, macramé, potting, weaving, holistic medicine, gin, cocaine, white wine, hash, Coors, Perrier, Dom Perignon, sunflower seeds, slippery elmroot. Nothing began in Aspen, but everything is there now. Everything.

Things are not always as clear as people would like them to be, of course. A man who raises cattle for a living in this time and place is an innocent. Costs soar, profits decline, and there's a man waiting down the road who'll pay $3 million for the ranch and turn it into a suburb. A man who walks through the countryside with his husky is an innocent too. It's a righteous thing to do. If the dog of the strolling innocent attacks and kills a calf belonging to the ranching innocent, and the ranching innocent, in turn, shoots the dog, are there any innocents left in the pasture? Or is the true innocent the man down the road who wants to buy the ranch for $3 million and turn it into a suburb?

Like America, Aspen suffers in 1980 from too much tinkering, from the impossible weight of too many contrary dreams and desires. Like America, it can't be more than it is. But we made it more than it is in our minds, and became angry when it didn't measure up. Like America, it has its own order. But we tried to overcome that order, and got angry when it resisted. Like America, Aspen is not done for, because it remains essentially intact, is still capable of rising to heights or sinking to depths not yet imagined. But in Aspen and America in 1980, the tinkerers prevail.

Loving the idea of something is much easier than loving the thing itself. It is also demeaning. The thing itself is what it is—limited, imperfect, specific. It is hard to love limited, imperfect, specific things. One must not only deal with the flaws, but accept the facts. In a way, one must love the flaws themselves. Loving the idea of the thing, on the other hand, is a snap. For the idea is what we want it to be and therefore unlimited, perfect, general.

The idea of Aspen, like the idea of America, was perfect. We came, we saw, we succumbed to the idea. But as time passed, we saw that the place itself was not perfect. The *place* hadn't changed. We had. When people live in an encouraging place, they grow more and more demanding, more and more sure of themselves. Hubris has always been Aspen's dominant quality because Aspen is an encouraging, benign, naturally generous place. People of a certain sort arrived in that high valley and said, "Oh my God, this is it. I am home at last." This should have been enough, but it wasn't. When one is given that much immediately, one eventually wants more. Aspen, having given us everything at the beginning, had no more to give. We began to think more of the idea of Aspen than the fact of Aspen. The idea overshadowed the reality, obscured it.

Aspen's innocence was, at first, circumstantial. Aspen had been kicked out of the game early, stayed on the sidelines for two generations, didn't participate at all in either the glory or the failures of America. Later, as it achieved some renown, its innocence became more calculated—innocence as imagined by the tinkerers and made manifest. Now it is vestigial, this innocence—a remnant, a leftover, and like all leftovers, incomplete. Aspen is a kind of professional innocent, but there is no such thing as professional innocence, so the people of Aspen are floundering.

Barnard and Pabst and their associates called what they did "progress." Edwards and Standley and their associates called what they did by other names, but it still looked like what was formerly called progress. No one has ever really defined progress. Innocents came to Aspen to escape America. In 1980 the Aspen they made attracts big-time buyers and sellers, wheelers and dealers, stars and tycoons. It has become an American capital. Perhaps that is what people mean when they speak of progress.

I see it more simply. I see the crankiness, the confusion, the bad moods of the people of Aspen as progress. Or growing pains anyway.

SOME PEOPLE complain that Aspen has been spoiled. Some of them live in Aspen and they mourn the passing of the halcyon days. Some of them live in other mountain towns in the West, and they vow that "what happened in Aspen" will never happen in their towns. Some are visitors who say each year with a kind of churlish satisfaction that everything is a little worse than it was last year. When Aspen became a capital, a star, some representatives of the press rushed to chronicle its decline. Others said that its success had gone to its head, made it vain. But there are still people who admire it, are moved by it in some way, find it intact and dazzling even after all these years.

Aspen has not been spoiled. It has not even changed. Aspen's story is not the familiar American success story: success spoils and absolute success spoils absolutely. What has happened in Aspen is as inevitable as winter and cannot be called good or bad any more than winter can be called good or bad. One can speak of hating winter or of loving it, but one cannot say that it is good or bad. Aspen is a fact—not good, not bad, just here and now.

When Walter Paepcke came to Aspen in 1945, he saw a town that was as dead as a town can be without being gone. He set about to revive it economically, physically and intellectually by using what was there and adding what was needed in nearly perfect proportions. He knew precisely what to do, and he did it very well. Those of us who lived there left everything to him in the way that lazy children leave everything to their father. He built a fine castle for us, with everything people might wish for in it, and then he died. Everything that happened after that was inevitable. The developers, the anti-growth movement, the popularity of the Aspen way of life, our way of life—each had to follow the other. It was only a matter of time—not if, but when.

Aspen in 1980 is what it always was, only it is larger. And its residents are what they always were, only more numerous. As a breed, we were not mean, and that was good. And we were amiable and rowdy, and that was not bad. But we were not rebels making a new world, we were rogues having a good time. In our innocence, we thought we were better than other people, but we were merely luckier. Those of us who came to Aspen to stay, from 1945 until 1980, have been less free spirits than errant spirits—all the class clowns, minor truants, pranksters and mildly wild ones come together for a long holiday in the mountains. We didn't want to grow up. And in Aspen we didn't have to. We withdrew from America—the fact, not the idea—not because it was crass or vile, but because it was boring and expected things from us. The ease of life in Aspen was as appealing to us as its beauty and freedom. Nature and time had made it beautiful. Walter Paepcke made it sound and interesting. We had to do nothing more than be present. We were less latter-day Thoreaus than we were perennial college students.

One of Aspen's most successful enterprises today is Aspen State Teachers College. It holds no classes, offers no degrees, employs no professors. It merely sells tee shirts, sweatshirts, hats, jackets, notebooks and all the other paraphernalia of collegiate life that the college seal can be printed on. Its nonexistent football team plays nongames against real opponents and always wins. Its humor magazine is a local best seller. It operates a bar called the Study Hall. Its enrollment continues to climb. One of its founders, Al Pendorf (aka Dean Fulton J. Begley), was interviewed on NBC by Tom Snyder. The old, old Aspen fantasy is a fact, and the fact is, of course, a fantasy.

We imposed our weaknesses on the place. In taking steps to protect it, we were really protecting ourselves. In celebrating the beauty of the place, we saw its fragility, and ignored its truth, its strength. We worried about how it looked, cherished its pretty vistas, and remained ignorant of how it worked, overlooking the complex, sound order of things. We passed endless ordinances, wrote complex zoning and planning codes, imposed extraordinary controls in the name of preservation, but at bottom, we were only trying to preserve ourselves. When we said we could "sell or save" Aspen, we meant we could sell or save ourselves.

Irony is as American as the proverbial apple pie, but less popular. Aspen is as American as apple pie, hot dogs and irony put together, and it is very popular. America admires our style. Everyone loves Huckleberry Finn, but no one loves Babbitt. There is in America, in its upper echelons anyway, a fear that when Huckleberry Finn grows up, he invariably turns into Babbitt. Huckleberry Finn is alive and well and living in Aspen . . . but Huckleberry Finn, like Babbitt, is a character in a novel, a fantasy, too. It is not clear yet whether anyone will live happily ever after.

American fantasies start in places like Aspen. They are shown on television and described in magazine articles. They are believed by more and more people and finally accepted as facts. In places like Aspen, someone declares nature to be not only superior to man but separate from him; someone else says that growth is destructive; and someone else says that the basic laws are not laws but clichés. In places like Aspen, people make up new rules for the old, old game, and their bravado is taken as proof that they are right. But fantasies are ephemeral at best. They fade and leave us face to face with the facts.

IT HAS BEEN SAID that Aspen has been sullied in some way, lost its purity. But it was never pure, for there is an abiding variousness to the Roaring Fork Valley. The relentless symmetry that astrophysicists speak of is the valley's central fact. It's a life of cycles, beginnings and ends, life and death. It has nothing to do with free enterprise, Democrats, the middle class, zoning, growth management, paradise. It has to do with heating and freezing, storming and shining, growing and dying. It has no fears, accepts all, folds it into the mix and does what it can with it.

Vast areas of the valley remain pastures, ranchlands or forests. One can walk a hundred yards into the woods and leave all that passes for civilization behind. Its floor seems constructed of cold, moldering old pine needles, leaves, broken branches, a primal damp. The trees reach up like pagan spires. The light is dim, holy, ancient, dusty. It is always cool there. Paths and roads of red and tan clay are deeply rutted and worn as smooth as old stones. Near their sources, mountain streams slap and rush high and clear in the early summer, become low and languid in the fall, iced and glamorous in the winter.

The high meadows are golden green in the summer, warm, wide and luxurious. They ride the mountains in the way a leaf rides the river. Here and there one finds crude old fences and cabins that time and weather are turning back into soil. The surface of the wood is dry, rough. Its interior is pulpy. In another two or three hundred years, the structures will be gone.

The ranches are tidier places, show a slow, slow struggle between men and the wilderness that will never end. They cut it back, it creeps forward. That is their role, and that is its role. Cattle stand as still as statues in the sun, flick their tails at flies from time to time. Horses run about, kick, whinny.

On the lower flanks of the mountains in certain canyons, in the acres of trees that stretch east from Aspen toward the Divide, there are clusters of houses that are not so much neighborhoods as they are clever compromises made between people and an untamed terrain full of dips and rises, juts and cavities.

Situated on a bluff overlooking Castle Creek, Snowbunny was Aspen's first and least felicitous suburb. But at its heart, there is, a lovely old cemetery full of tall trees, shadows, polished headstones and worn statues.

In 1889 an artist drew a bird's-eye-view map of Aspen, each house no bigger than a monogram, but drawn meticulously. Then as now Aspen's West End was a spacious and supreme neighborhood. The West End is popular. In 1980 its houses rarely sell for less than $300,000. Comparable houses would cost $50,000 somewhere else. Some people have lived there for fifty years in houses that fit them like clothes. There are snappier people, too, who go about in tennis whites and handsome jogging costumes. Their teeth are very white. A daughter of financier Paul Mellon, the lead singer of the rock group Chicago and actor Jack Nicholson each bought one of the large old Victorian houses. Their three houses face each other across a small park. The neighbors haven't decided whether they like the newcomers. Elizabeth Paepcke's large Victorian house looks onto the park too. In 1945 Albert Schweitzer and Gary Cooper. In 1980 Mrs. Paepcke, a Mellon, a rock star, a leading man. America is wonderful. Aspen is wonderful.

The Victorian houses, some small and shabby, some large and immaculate, some mere imitations, have absorbed a scattering of modern houses so completely that the neighborhood remains resolutely Victorian. Its residents battle passionately to keep it intact, are critical of any apparent violation of their notion of things. The West Side Civic Association is very busy.

Tall old cottonwood trees line the streets. Some of them are dying because the city has neglected the irrigation ditches that sustained the trees, and the thirst of a cottonwood tree is enormous. Residents hector city officials about the trees, and officials promise to restore the ditches, but the trees are dying.

On the north rim of the West End, a hundred feet below, is Hallam Lake. Beyond it is the Roaring Fork. Beyond it Red Mountain. On its broad lower flanks are extravagant modern houses whose windows flash rudely in the late afternoon sun, diamonds in the rough. They are a vivid expression of affluence, showy, melodramatic. West End residents thank God they do not live in any of those houses.

The tent, the Aspen Institute buildings, the Aspen Center for Physics and the Given Institute for Pathobiology are all situated in the West End. One can encounter Nobel Prize winners in the road, world-famous violinists, or Mortimer Adler.

Downtown Aspen has grown large enough to fill the night sky with a soft pink light. One sees many sorts of people there, many enterprises. There are bookstores and galleries, a shop that sells strong teas and Dunhill cigarettes, store windows full of formidable sheepskin coats. A restaurant in an old bank, another with a wall of browning photos of boxers in tights. A store where one can buy copper pans from France and brass miners' lamps from Wales, stores that sell fancy used clothes, a Hallmark gift store, a Baskin Robbins and more boutiques than one can count.

The mall, with its stream and flowers and trees in summer and its artful snowbanks in the winter, is like a movie set. At one end children hang like ornaments off a massive timber structure. Beyond, in Wagner Park, men and women play rugby, softball, soccer and volleyball.

Main Street is something like those slices of rock in which a geologist reads an entire history. One can walk its length in fifteen minutes. Pitkin County Courthouse, the Hotel Jerome, and several large, exquisitely kept Victorian houses tell of a people with fervent material ambitions. The false-front *Aspen Times* building and Mesa Store building suggest a more raffish sort of citizen. St. Mary's Church with its tall pinched rectory seems the creation of a furious and devout people. Motels and lodges try in various ways, mostly raucous, to outshine each other, calling to mind a group of fretful managers. A modern brick emulation of the stately courthouse, a gas station and a bank composed of geometric shapes and long curves and a hectic neo-Victorian building seem made by people anxious to be simultaneously tasteful and commercial. Old shambling Victorian houses— one a Chinese restaurant, the other something called "Inner Gardens"—demonstrate an adaptable people. The Pitkin County Library, a nearby bookstore and a blizzard of frisbees over Paepcke Park affirm the presence of devotees of art and sport.

In the late afternoon, visitors of all ages, from many places, hurry along Main Street and speak of the wonderful things that await them in downtown Aspen.

Crowded near the base of Smuggler Mountain, just northeast of the city, are Silver King Apartments and the Smuggler Trailer Court. They house hundreds of young people and workers. At "Silver Slum," as it is sometimes called, people kick in doors from time to time, or put their fists through walls. Some speak in obscenities of city leaders, tourists, "greedheads." Soon they will be gone. Silver King has been bought by a developer, will be improved, turned into condominiums.

Silver King is a ten-minute walk from the West End, visible from Hunter Creek where the first prospectors camped on their way to Aspen. By any measure but man's, a hundred years is a very short time. To a place caught in a time warp, it is no time at all.

One hundred years old but hardly showing its age, Aspen offers America, which is two hundred years old and looking older now, pleasure and absolution all at once.

In the eighteenth century, America made itself. In the nineteenth century, it made itself rich. In the twentieth century, it made itself powerful. Then it thought, as the rich and powerful often do, "There must be more to life than this."

Out of time, out of step, Aspen played at sport and art and even politics. Having a wonderful time, America, wish you were here. Look at us, America, we are skiing down mountains, ripping up our streets, thumbing our nose at progress, making politics amusing. We're having our way, America, and you're not. We're young and free, and you're not. We have neither smog, nor slums, nor hamburger stands, nor crowded throughways, nor angry minorities.

America came to Aspen, and life came along with it, and life became the main game. It seems to consist of est, jogging and real estate. In the first year of the 1980s, the game palls, and the players, in time, in step now, are out of sorts. Like America, they are not ready to give up their innocence.

Aspen can break your heart. Most of the leading players got burned. Walter Paepcke died too soon. Herbert Bayer sold his Aspen house to Claudine Longet. He comes to Aspen in the summers now, but lives in Santa Barbara. D. R. C. Brown moved back to his ranch in Carbondale. Fred Glidden is dead. Bob Craig ran an advertising design firm in Denver for a while, then went on to set up a program very much like the Institute at Keystone, another Colorado mountain resort. He insists that Bob Anderson is a good man, a genius. He published a book about his most recent mountain climbing experience. It ended tragically. Shorty Pabst still owns property in Pitkin County, but moved back to Wisconsin to live. Bugsy Barnard lives in Silt, still agitating for this or that. Ned Vare moved from his ranch in Silt to a house in Glenwood Springs. Hunter Thompson still lives in Woody Creek, but works on the Coasts, East and West. He's writing movies now, and an occasional magazine article. Dwight Shellman continues to be the leading legal advocate of unrestrained growth. "The Hanging Judge," John Wendt, rides to the hounds in Paonia, Colorado. Stacy Standley chose not to run for a fourth term as mayor. The new mayor, Herman Edel, a successful businessman, has no business interests in Aspen. Joe Edwards has been heard to say that he might run for Congress. Bil Dunaway still covers the city council and recites their own history to them from time to time, but he talks more of tennis. Fritz Benedict remains busy, happy and optimistic. Recent projects include a mammoth shopping center at Snowmass Resort, and a multimillion-dollar plan for downtown Aspen.

Innocence, like pimples and puppy love, is something to be gone through and got over, a stage, not a state. One cannot make a life out of it, anymore than a life can be made of tinsel and cotton candy. Held onto too long, it goes bad, sour, dangerous. But the game goes on in Aspen. Many of the players may no longer have the heart for it, but they don't know how to end it. Aspen is a dazzling arena, and America, grateful for the diversion, stays on.

Leaving Eldorado

F OR ME it ended as suddenly as it had begun.
    In 1953 I went to Aspen for the summer, returned
to New York in the fall, and was so homesick for Aspen
that I went back to stay two months later. In 1979 I went
to Philadelphia for the winter, stayed six months instead
of three, returned to Aspen in July, and was so homesick
for Philadelphia that I went back to stay two months later.

It was, of course, more complicated than that. These
giant interior shifts are not simple. A friend said, "You're
not really leaving Aspen, you're just moving to Philadelphia." It was a comfortable notion, and I smiled agreea-
bly, but it was not true. I was leaving Aspen.

The day I left, I walked out in the early morning one
last time. The mountains looked wonderful, but my eyes
were on the distant edge of things. I went back to my
house, had breakfast, packed plate, cup, silver and skil-
let, and taped the last box closed. There was nothing left
to do but go.

A friend came by to take me to the airport. As I tossed
my rucksack and trenchcoat into his car, he said, "This
is certainly unceremonious." It was. I did not look back
or cry or say anything memorable. Because whatever it
was, it was finished.

When life caught up with us in Aspen, we made a game of it, as we had done with sport and art and politics and nature. But I had no interest in est, jogging or real estate, and went in search of real life; went back, not surprisingly, to where I had left it twenty-five years before, back to a big old eastern city. Life, being generous, forgiving and ungrudging, held out its hand to me—in all its fast, odd, mundane glory—and I seized it.

Then too, if America had come to Aspen, there seemed no point in not going back to America, the real thing, where, as a friend of mine said, "Real Italians sell the sausage." In Aspen, we demanded pretty views from every window. In America, in Philadelphia, light is enough.

PHILADELPHIANS do not fear black shoes or worship ten-speed bikes. They are not mellow or laid back. Every day, one of them overcomes something—sleet, heat, a rackety bus, a derailed train, a mean cop, a crazy, a store clerk who refuses to help, a truck driver who wants you off the road, a hardhat yelling obscenities. Philadelphians are so busy trying to make it through the day that they have no time to brood over such ephemeral questions as happiness and fulfillment. When they get home at the end of another brutal day on the lines, they grin, and the grin says, "I made it again." That grin at the end of the day is often exhausted, sometimes slow in coming, but it is the real thing, and it is wonderful to see. Such people are a comfort and a challenge all at once.

Life in Philadelphia is something like life in a war zone. Unspeakable things happen. A woman was beaten to death with a toilet seat a thousand feet from where I was sleeping. Several days later, several thousand feet away, a bar owner was beaten insensible with a pipe and

robbed. It was a Sunday morning. Brunch would be
served a little later. The son of friends was terrorized on
a subway by a gang of boys. A friend was mugged on his
way home from a party. Another friend's house was broken into and robbed three times in three months.

Startling things happen. I came home one day to find
that the hall stairway in my building was gone. I couldn't
get into my apartment on the second floor until late that
evening when a new stairway was more or less in place.
There had been no notice. Recently I returned home
after several days in New York to find a terrible white
dust all over the hallway. Soon it was all over me, and
now it is all over my apartment. I don't know what it is.

There are five other tenants in my building. I have
been coming and going for months, and I have never
seen two of them. It is not a big building, is a Colonial
house in fact. We share a hall, stairs, doors. They live only
inches from me but I know nothing about them—except
that the one below has been told at least twice that she
does not "relate well to people." One of the tenants I
knew said one day that he was "off to Florida." I never
saw him again.

I am more in touch with life on the street than with
life under my own roof. Car doors slam, people sing,
shout at one another, make deals, break appointments,
run, stumble. There are a great many sirens. In the windows of the houses across the street, I see shadows, light,
plants, books, corners of paintings, a naked man. The
trees outside my windows have a life of their own. The
shouts, the sirens, the slamming doors, the trees, the
naked man all suggest that life in the war zone is ram-
bunctious and wearing.

Proofs are all around. Friends vanish into funks. A fat
woman steps on your foot and scolds you. An old man

shouts Polish obscenities at you one day, smiles in a courtly way the next. The kid at the drugstore finishes combing his hair before taking your money. Some days the beer is warm and the spaghetti is cold.

But as in war zones, people stay on the lines and reach out to one another and hold on, friends and strangers alike. I walk every morning and pass the same people regularly. If I'm absent for several days, when I show up again, they say, "You O.K.? When we don't see you, we worry, you know."

City life requires patience, daring and exquisite timing. A hundred times a day, if one were a step ahead or behind, one could be killed by a car, slammed into a wall, crushed in an elevator door. On the streets an endless and extraordinarily intricate ballet takes place as millions of people rush here and there. Only a handful are killed or maimed, testifying to the skill and compassion of the dancers. City life uses you up daily. Whatever you have, whatever you are, it uses all of it, and there is a kind of pleasure in that.

Philadelphia is America's fourth largest city. Nearly two million people live within its bounds. It is situated between two rivers, the graceful Schuykill and the big Delaware. One sees slim boys rowing light shells on the Schuykill, gigantic freighters on the Delaware. Though it is eighty miles from the sea, Philadelphia is the largest fresh-water port in the world. Freighters from Russia, Australia, everywhere, move up the Delaware, berth under giant cranes, unload, reload, move down the river again. On some mornings the river stinks, but most mornings it smells like the sea. Its tides are irregular. Sailboats, tiny fast motorboats, tugs, barges, yachts and ducks, as well as freighters, ride the tides. I live two blocks from the Delaware.

There is a statue of William Penn, the maker of the city, on top of city hall. His hat is forty stories up, and no building can be taller than his hat. There are many tall buildings—forty stories is plenty tall, I think—but there are hundreds of thousands of small buildings. From Billy Penn's hat, Philadelphia looks as intricate as a jigsaw puzzle, each piece joining the other neatly. It is a city of neighborhoods, as someone said. Queen Village, Society Hill, Old City, Olney, the Great Northeast, South Philly. In the neighborhoods, there are townhouses or row houses. They have wonderful roofs pitched this way and that, full of juts and dives, dormer windows, chimneys, TV antennas poking up from surfaces of tin, shingle, tar, are red, brown, black, green, blue. It looks orderly and serene from Billy Penn's hat.

At street level the city looks less orderly. One moves in a blink from an elegant street onto a mess of a street —stores boarded up, windows kicked in, broken glass glittering in the weeds. Only the graffiti is up to date: "Trash is truth." The city is still moored around Billy Penn's rational grid and some of it still resembles "the greene country towne" he made, with its spacious squares, trees, cobblestone streets, brick sidewalks, trim townhouses with white marble steps, black wrought-iron railings, shutters. But some of it looks like the war has been lost to rubble, sadness, and rage.

America was invented in Philadelphia. Franklin, Adams, Jefferson—the principal inventors—walked on the cobblestone streets I walk on, worked in rooms I have entered. There are thrilling airs in those rooms. America is being re-invented here daily, though there is more improvisation now than invention. It is a messy, noisy, spirited process. I think it will end well.

A fragment of a Tom Waits song was in my head when

I took off on Aspen Airways that last time and it was still in my head when I landed in Philadelphia five hours later. "The sun's comin' up. I'm ridin' with Lady Luck. Freeway cars and trucks . . ."

When it snows in Philadelphia, I ache a little. Not because I miss Aspen, but because I don't. I miss certain specific vistas, certain people, and I miss those fine easy moments that one can have only with very old friends, but I do not miss Aspen.

Not long ago, I saw an ad in the *New York Times.* It said, "Aspen is a party and you're invited." I spent half my life at the party and one day I went out to get some air and didn't go back. Perhaps I grew up and Aspen didn't. Perhaps I changed and it didn't. In any case, I am here and it is still out there, and neither of us, Aspen or me, is innocent anymore. I think that's a good thing, but I no longer speak for Aspen, only for myself.